TABLE OF CONTEN

Copyright Law Guidebook
What Every Writer Should Know About Intellectual Property Rights

DISCLAIMER AND TERMS OF USE AGREEMENT:

(Please Read This Before Using This Book)

This information is for educational and informational purposes only. The content is not intended to be a substitute for any professional advice, diagnosis, or treatment.

The author and publisher of this book and the accompanying materials have used their best efforts in preparing this book.

The author and publisher make no representation or warranties with respect to the accuracy, applicability, fitness, or completeness of the contents of this book. The information contained in this book is strictly for educational purposes. Therefore, if you wish to apply ideas contained in this book, you are taking full responsibility for your actions.

The author and publisher disclaim any warranties (express or implied), merchantability, or fitness for any particular purpose. The author and publisher shall in no event be held liable to any party for any direct, indirect, punitive, special, incidental or other consequential damages arising directly or indirectly from any use of this material, which is provided “as is”, and without

Introduction – The Right to Protect Intellectual Property

At the time of this writing, if I were asked what topic authors and writers know the least about, it would be a toss-up between International Standard Book Numbers (ISBNs) and copyright laws.

I solved the problem about ISBNs with my book, "International Standard Book Numbers" http://www.amazon.com/dp/B00B2YB4SK and now, with this book, "Copyright Law Guidebook", I wish to solve the other problem that authors and writers know the least about.

As with most books, I cannot answer all of an author's/writer's questions so I have provided an online link to a website where you can ask any copyright question and a copyright attorney will answer it for free. Go here:

http://tinyurl.com/ask-copyrightquestion

I have also provided an online link to the US Government's Copyright Resource page where you can download any report for free, all of which are designed to give you the complete information on copyrights laws. Go here:

http://www.copyright.gov/title17/

Here is what the library of document resources includes:

Complete version of the U.S. Copyright Law, December 2011 [PDF format = 2 Mb]

- Preface: Amendments to Title 17 since 1976
- Chapter 1: Subject Matter and Scope of Copyright
- Chapter 2: Copyright Ownership and Transfer
- Chapter 3: Duration of Copyright
- Chapter 4: Copyright Notice, Deposit, and Registration
- Chapter 5: Copyright Infringement and Remedies
- Chapter 6: Importation and Exportation
- Chapter 7: Copyright Office
- Chapter 8: Proceedings by Copyright Royalty Judges
- Chapter 9: Protection of Semiconductor Chip Products
- Chapter 10: Digital Audio Recording Devices and Media
- Chapter 11: Sound Recordings and Music Videos
- Chapter 12: Copyright Protection and Management Systems
- Chapter 13: Protection of Original Designs
- Appendix A: The Copyright Act of 1976
- Appendix B: The Digital Millennium Copyright Act of 1998
- Appendix C: The Copyright Royalty and Distribution Reform Act of 2004
- Appendix D: The Satellite Home Viewer Extension and

Reauthorization Act of 2004

- Appendix E: The Intellectual Property Protection and Courts Amendments Act of 2004
- Appendix F: The Prioritizing Resources and Organization for Intellectual Property Act of 2008
- Appendix G: The Satellite Television Extension and Localism Act of 2010
- Appendix H: Title 18 — Crimes and Criminal Procedure, U. S. Code
- Appendix I: Title 28 — Judiciary and Judicial Procedure, U. S. Code
- Appendix J: Title 44 — Public Printing and Documents, U. S. Code
- Appendix K: The Berne Convention Implementation Act of 1988
- Appendix L: The Uruguay Round Agreements Act of 1994
- Appendix M: GATT/Trade-Related Aspects of Intellectual Property Rights (TRIPs) Agreement, Part II
- Appendix N: Definition of "Berne Convention Work

It is important to have available all of the government resources available on copyright laws. Go here:

http://www.copyright.gov/laws/

I also want to make you aware of a very unique website if you are a graphic designer, do logos, websites, etc. This site offers you not only a marketplace where buyers come to hire your services, but also protects your creative works using some of the strongest copyright software available today. Check it out here:

http://www.crowdspring.com/

Note: CrowdSpring is not for authors and writers.

Copyright Law involves many facets and provides protection for many classifications considered Intellectual property. This book covers just about every form of intellectual property cited within the federal code but if I have missed anything please feel free to write to me. My in-house copyright attorneys will respond.

I welcome your questions. Write to me: lee.benton@epubwealth.com

Okay, let's get at it…

Chapter 1 – Copyright Basics

I want to begin by providing you with the basics when it some to Copyright Law. The important things to an author is when is their works covered and how long it lasts as well as what does it cost, etc. This section will answer these questions and more. The following article really gets to the meat of the questions…

http://www.copyright.com/Services/copyrightoncampus/basics/law.html

Copyright protection exists from the moment a work is created in a fixed, tangible form of expression. The copyright *immediately* becomes the property of the author who created the work. Only the author, or those deriving their rights through the author, can rightfully claim copyright. In the case of works made for hire, the employer—not the writer—is considered the author.

The First Sale Doctrine

The physical ownership of an item such as a book, painting, manuscript or CD is not the same as owning the copyright to the work embodied in that item.

Under the First Sale Doctrine (Section 109 of the Copyright Act), ownership of a physical copy of a copyright-protected work permits lending, reselling, disposing, etc., of the item. However, it does not permit reproducing the material, publicly displaying or performing it, or engaging in any of the acts reserved for the copyright holder.

Why?

Because the transfer of the physical copy does not transfer the copyright holder's rights to the work. Even including an attribution on a copied work (for example, putting the author's name on it) does not eliminate the need to obtain the copyright holder's consent. To use copyrighted materials lawfully, you must secure permission from the applicable copyright holders or a copyright licensing agent.

Duration of Copyright

The term of copyright protection depends upon the date of creation. A work created on or after January 1, 1978, is ordinarily protected by copyright from the moment of its creation until 70 years after the author's death.

For works made for hire, anonymous works and pseudonymous works (unless the author's identity is revealed in Copyright Office records), the duration of copyright is 95 years from publication or 120 years from creation, whichever is shorter.

For works created, published or registered before January 1, 1978, or for more detailed information, you may wish to refer to the public domain section of this guide or request Circular 15 ("Renewal of Copyright"), Circular 15a ("Duration of

Copyright") and Circular 15t ("Extension of Copyright Terms") from the U.S. Copyright Office Website, www.copyright.gov.

Registration and Notification of Copyright

The way in which copyright protection is secured is frequently misunderstood. Copyright is secured ***automatically*** when the work is created and fixed in a tangible form, such as the first time it is written or recorded. No other action is required to secure copyright protection – neither publication, registration nor other action in the Copyright Office (although registration is recommended).

IMPORTANT: The use of a copyright notice is no longer required under U.S. law, although it is recommended. This requirement was eliminated when the United States adhered to the Berne Convention effective March 1, 1989. If a copyright holder wants to use a copyright notice, he or she may do so freely without permission from or registration with the U.S. Copyright Office. In fact, the use of a copyright notice is recommended because it reminds the public that the work is protected by copyright.

A copyright notice should contain all the following three elements:

1. The symbol © (the letter C in a circle), the word "Copyright" or the abbreviation "Copr."
2. The year when the work was first created.
3. The name of the owner of the copyright.

Example: © 2005 John Doe

Public Domain

The public domain comprises all works that are either no longer protected by copyright or never were. It should not be confused with the mere fact that a work is publicly available (such as information in books or periodicals, or content on the Internet).

Essentially, all works first published in the United States before 1923 are considered to be in the public domain in the United States. The public domain also extends to works published between 1923 and 1963 on which copyright registrations were not renewed.

All materials created since 1989, except those created by the U.S. federal government, are presumptively protected by copyright. As a result, the chances are high that the materials of greatest interest to students and faculty are not in the public domain. In addition, you must also consider other forms of legal protection such as trademark or patent protection before reusing third-party content.

Public domain materials generally fall into one of four categories:

1. Generic information such as facts, numbers and ideas.
2. Works whose copyrights have lapsed over time or whose copyright holders have failed to renew a registration (a requirement that applies to works created before 1978).
3. Works published before March 1989 that failed to include a proper notice of copyright.
4. Works created by the U.S. federal government.

In rare instances, works may also be "dedicated" (i.e., donated) to the public domain.

Penalties of Copyright Infringement

By reproducing, republishing or redistributing the work of a copyright holder without permission, you may be violating or infringing on his or her rights under the Copyright Act.

If the copyright holder has registered the work with the U.S. Copyright Office prior to the infringement, the copyright holder may sue for compensation. Court-ordered compensation may include damages such as lost profits from the infringing activity or statutory damages ranging from $250 to $150,000, plus attorneys' fees, for each infringing copy. Even higher damages may be awarded if the court feels that the infringement was committed "willfully."

You may also be criminally liable if you willfully copy a work for profit or financial gain, or if the copied work has a value of more than $1,000. In these cases, penalties can include a one-year jail sentence plus fines. If the value is more than $2,500, you may be sentenced to five years in jail plus fines. Criminal penalties generally apply to large-scale commercial piracy.

"International" Copyright

There is no such thing as an "international" copyright that automatically protects a work throughout the world. However, the most widely-adopted copyright treaty, the Berne Convention, states that once a work is protected in one of the Convention member countries, it is protected by copyright in all of them. As of mid-2004, 156 countries, including the U.S., belong to the Berne Convention.

The Berne Convention further states that the scope and limitations of any copyright are based upon the laws of the country where the misuse of the copyright-protected work takes place (rather than the country where the work originated). For example, if you photocopy an article in the U.S., then U.S. copyright law applies to determine whether that copy was lawful. Similarly, if you digitize an image in the UK, the copyright laws of the UK apply to determine whether that digitized use is lawful.

There are grey areas, however, when it comes to the online usage of copyright-protected content. For example, if an article is uploaded in the U.S. and then viewed on a Website in Australia, where is the "copying" taking place – and is more than one "copy" being made? Courts in the U.S. and around the world have yet to provide definitive answers as to what country's laws should be used to determine online copyright infringement in this case. To avoid a potential legal challenge from the copyright holder, many institutions follow a policy of "when in doubt, obtain permission" in these situations.

What is Copyright Protected?

http://www.copyright.com/Services/copyrightoncampus/basics/law_protected.html

Copyright-Protected

- Literary works
- Musical works, including any accompanying words
- Dramatic works, including any accompanying music
- Pantomimes and choreographic works
- Pictorial, graphic and sculptural works
- Motion pictures and other audiovisual works
- Sound recordings

Not Copyright-Protected

- Works that have not been fixed in a tangible form of expression by being written, recorded or captured electronically.
- Titles, names, short phrases and slogans; familiar symbols or designs; mere variations of typographic ornamentation, lettering or coloring; mere listings of ingredients or contents.
- Ideas, facts, data, procedures, methods, systems, processes, concepts, principles, discoveries or devices, as distinguished from a description, explanation or illustration.
- Works consisting entirely of information that are natural or

- Architectural works
- Computer software

self-evident facts, containing no original authorship, such as the white pages of telephone books, standard calendars, height and weight charts and tape measures and rulers.

- Works created by the U.S. Government.
- Works for which copyright has expired; works in the public domain.

When Works Pass into the Public Domain

http://www.copyright.com/Services/copyrightoncampus/basics/law_public.html

Date of Work	Protected From	Term
Created 1-1-78 or after	As soon as the work is fixed in a tangible medium of expression	Life + 70 years[1] (or in the case of corporate authorship, the shorter of 95 years from publication or 120 years from creation[2])
Published before 1923	In public domain	None
Published from 1923 - 63	When published with notice[3]	28 years plus the option to renew for another 67 years. If not so renewed, it is now in the public domain
Published	When published	28 years for the first

from 1964 - 77	with notice[3]	term, plus an automatic extension of 67 years for the second term
Created before 1-1-78 but not published	1-1-78, the effective date of the 1976 Act which eliminated common law copyright	Life + 70 years or 12-31-2002, whichever is later
Created before 1-1-78 Published between then and 12-31-2002	1-1-78, the effective date of the 1976 Act which eliminated common law copyright	Life + 70 years or 12-31-2047, whichever is later

[1] The term of joint works is measured by the life of the longest-lived author.
[2] Works for hire, anonymous and pseudonymous works also have this term. 17 U.S.C. § 302(c).
[3] Under the 1909 Copyright Act, works published without notice went into the public domain upon publication. Works published without notice between 1-1-78 and 3-1-89 (the effective date of the Berne Convention Implementation Act) retained copyright protection only if an effort to correct the accidental omission of notice was made within five years, such as by placing notice on unsold copies. 17 U.S.C. § 405.

Copyright Basics: Fair Use

http://www.copyright.com/Services/copyrightoncampus/basics/fairuse.html

Fair use is a concept embedded in U.S. law that recognizes that certain uses of copyright-protected works do not require permission from the copyright holder or its agent. These include instances of minimal use that do not interfere with the copyright holder's exclusive rights to reproduce and reuse the work.

Fair use is not an exception to copyright compliance; it is more of a "legal defense." That is, if you copy and share a copyright-protected work and the copyright holder claims copyright infringement, you may be able to assert a defense of fair use which you would then have to prove.

Fair use is primarily intended to allow the use of copyright-protected works for commentary, parody, news reporting, research and education. **However, not all uses in an academic context are automatically considered fair use.**

The Copyright Act does not spell out the specific types of content reproduction that qualify as fair use. It offers an outline as to how to analyze whether fair use may apply in a particular situation.

As a result, the Copyright Act leaves it up to the individual to determine, based upon the factors in Section 107 of the Act, whether fair use applies in each particular circumstance. To avoid a potential legal challenge from the copyright holder, many institutions follow a policy of "when in doubt, obtain permission."

Determining Fair Use

Section 107 of the Copyright Act lists four factors to help you determine types of content usage that may be considered fair use. No one factor alone dictates whether a particular use is indeed fair use. Consideration of all four factors is needed to help determine whether or not copyright permission is required.

Before applying these factors to your situation, identify if the use is for **criticism, comment, news reporting, education, scholarship or research**. If the answer is no, obtain copyright permission to use the content. If the answer is yes, examine the four factors listed below.

1. **The purpose and character of the use, including whether it is for commercial use or for nonprofit educational purposes.** In evaluating the purpose and character of the use, courts favor non-profit educational uses over commercial ones. However, there are instances in which commercial uses would qualify as fair use and other instances where educational uses would not meet the criteria. Courts also favor productive uses that yield a "transformational" result. Thus, extensive quoting from a work to produce a critical analysis of that work is favored over "slavish copying" that merely reproduces a copyrighted work.
2. **The nature of the copyrighted work.** This factor focuses on the work itself. The legislative history states that there is a definite difference between reproducing a short news note and reproducing a full musical score because of the nature of the work. Moreover, some works, such as standardized tests and workbooks, will never qualify for fair use because by their nature they are meant to be consumed. Uses of factual works such as scientific articles are more likely to fall within fair use.
3. **The amount and substantiality of the portion used in relation to the copyright-protected work as a whole.** This factor considers how much of the copyrighted work was used in comparison to the original work as a whole. Generally, the larger the amount used, the less likely a court will find the use to be a fair use. Amount and substantiality is also a qualitative test; that is, even though one takes only a small portion of a work, it still may be too much if what is taken is the "heart of the work."
4. **The effect of the use on the potential market for or value of the copyright-protected work.** Courts use this factor to determine whether the use of a work is likely to result in an economic loss that the copyright

holder is otherwise entitled to receive. It looks at whether the nature of the use competes with or diminishes the potential market for the use that the owner is already exploiting or can reasonably be expected soon to exploit. Even if the immediate loss is not substantial, courts have found that, should the loss become great if the practice were to become widespread, then this factor favors the copyright holder.

While these four factors are helpful guides, they do not clearly identify uses that are or are not fair use. Fair use is not a straightforward concept; therefore, any fair use analysis must be conducted on a case-by-case basis considering all four factors and the circumstances of the situation at hand.

Examples of Fair Use:

- Quotation of short passages in a scholarly or technical work for illustration or clarification of the author's observations.
- Spontaneous and unexpected reproduction of material for classroom use–for example, where an article in the morning's paper is directly relevant to that day's class topic.
- A parody that includes short portions of a work.
- A summary of an address or article, which may include quotations of short passages of the copyright-protected work.

Understanding the scope of fair use—and becoming familiar with those situations where it is more likely to apply and those where it is less likely to—can help guard you and your institution from an infringement claim due to the unauthorized use of copyright-protected materials.

Copyright Compliance Policies often provide faculty, staff, students and others with guidelines for fair use, although there will always be exceptions, such as the exceptions for libraries and archives, exceptions for the use of materials in an educational setting and the guidelines for classroom copying.

Exceptions for Libraries and Archives

Section 108 of the Copyright Act provides specific exceptions for libraries and archives in which they may make reproductions without obtaining permission from, or providing compensation to, the copyright holder.

To qualify for the exception, your library or archive must:

- Produce no more than a single reproduction of a given work.
- Derive no commercial gain from the reproduction.
- Be open to the general public or to persons researching the specialized area in the library collection.
- Include a notice of copyright or, in the absence of a notice on the work copied, a note that the work may be protected under copyright law.

In these instances, reproduction is meant to be isolated and unrelated; it should not result in the related or concerted reproduction of the same materials over a period of time. Neither should reproduction be systematic and serve as a substitute for a subscription to or purchase of the original work.

Reproduction under the exception may be done for the purpose of:

- **Library user requests for articles and short excerpts.** At the request of a library user or another library on behalf of a library user, your library or archive may make one reproduction of an article from a periodical or a small part of any other work. The reproduction must become the property of the library user. The library must have no reason to believe that the reproduction will be used for purposes other than private study, scholarship and research. The library must also display the register's notice at the place where library users make their reproduction requests.

- **Archival reproductions of unpublished works.** Up to three reproductions of any unpublished work may be made for preservation, security or deposit for research use in another library or archive. This may be a photocopy or digital reproduction. If it is a digital reproduction, it may not be made available to the public outside the library or archive premises. Prior to making the reproduction, your library or archive must make a reasonable effort to purchase a new replacement at a fair price. The library or archive must also own the work in its collection before reproducing it.
- **Replacement of lost, damaged or obsolete copies.** Your library or archive may make up to three reproductions (including digital copies) of a published work that is lost, stolen, damaged, deteriorating or stored in an obsolete format. Any digital reproductions must be kept within the confines of the library (that is, available on its computer but not placed on a public network).
- **Library user requests for entire works.** If certain conditions are met, your library may make one reproduction of an entire book or periodical at the request of either a library user or another library on behalf of a user. The library must first determine after reasonable investigation that a reproduction cannot be obtained at a reasonable price. The reproduction must become the property of the library user. The library must have no reason to believe that the reproduction will be used for purposes other than private study, scholarship and research. Finally, the library must display the register's notice at the place in the library where users make their reproduction requests.

Exceptions for the Use of Materials in an Educational Setting

Section 110 of the Copyright Act outlines provisions for the performance and display of copyright-protected content in the classroom so long as certain requirements are met.

Section 110 (1) allows for the performance and display of copyright-protected works in face-to-face classroom settings, with some specific limitations related to the use of motion pictures.

Section 110 (2) applies to distance education, including any situation where students receive materials through digital transmission.

Requirements for the use of copyright-protected content in distance education:

- Be an accredited, non-profit educational institution.
- Develop and implement copyright policies.
- Provide students with information on copyright laws and compliance.
- Notify students that course materials may be subject to copyright protection.
- Use technical controls that limit access to copyright-protected content to enrolled students and that prevent storage and dissemination of copyright-protected works.

Permitted uses of copyright-protected content in the distance education:

- Performances of non-dramatic literary and musical works.
- Performances of "reasonable and limited portions" of any other type of work.

The TEACH Act amended sections 110(2) and 112(f) for distance learning.

Copyright Basics: The Digital Millennium Copyright Act

The Digital Millennium Copyright Act (DMCA) (pdf) was passed into law in 1998 to address some of the issues unique to digital copyright. In order to help copyright holders protect their digital content, the DMCA contains provisions forbidding circumvention of digital protections and protecting copyright management information.

The anti-circumvention provisions prohibit the unauthorized circumvention of technological measures which control access to or restrict the use of a copyright-protected work. Such technological measures may involve a password or encryption; breaking the password or encryption is illegal.

Copyright management information includes the title of a work, the name of the author or copyright holder and other identifying information. Intentionally removing or altering such information violates a provision of the DMCA.

The DMCA provides limited liability for university networks acting as Internet service providers (ISPs) for students and faculty, provided that certain requirements are met.

Requirements of the DMCA:

- Appoint a designated agent to receive reports of copyright infringement. Register the agent with the U.S. Copyright Office.
- Develop and post a copyright policy. Educate campus community about copyright.
- Comply with "take down" requests.
- Apply measures to protect against unauthorized access to content and dissemination of information.
- Use only lawfully acquired copies of copyrighted works.

Chapter 2 – How To Copyright For FREE

Copyrighting, on the most part, is free. There are circumstances where you will wish to seek a copyright attorney's advice but this flows along the lines of other types of intellectual property pother than written content. The following article offers a quick guide to immediate copyrighting and applies to all authors.

http://www.ehow.com/how_4483477_copyright.html

The best way to protect your creativity -- stuff like writing, photos, music, clever titles, names, websites, business ideas, software and other creative output -- is with copyright, which you can do absolutely free. You might need other intellectual property protection as well, but most copyright protections are free and automatic.

To repeat from Chapter 1:

The way in which copyright protection is secured is frequently misunderstood. Copyright is secured ***automatically*** when the work is created and fixed in a tangible form, such as the first time it is written or recorded. No other action is required to secure copyright protection – neither publication, registration nor other action in the Copyright Office (although registration is recommended).

IMPORTANT: The use of a copyright notice is no longer required under U.S. law, although it is recommended. This requirement was eliminated when the United States adhered to the Berne Convention effective March 1, 1989. If a copyright holder wants to use a copyright notice, he or she may do so freely without permission from or registration with the U.S. Copyright Office. In fact, the use of a copyright notice is recommended because it reminds the public that the work is protected by copyright.

A copyright notice should contain all the following three elements:

1. The symbol © (the letter C in a circle), the word "Copyright" or the abbreviation "Copr."
2. The year when the work was first created.
3. The name of the owner of the copyright.

Example: © 2005 John Doe

Instructions to file a copyright:

1. Head to the U.S. Copyright Office's FAQs page at http://www.copyright.gov. The Copyright Office is part of the Library of Congress. This is your best source of information.
2. Note that copyright is automatic and happens from the simple act of creating a written product. The moment you create something, it's protected by US copyright law.
3. Understand what is protected by copyright. Many things are protected by copyright, including written materials, lyrics, music, software, photographs, drawings and websites.

4. Understand what is not protected by copyright, including names, titles, simple recipes, short phrases, and ideas.
5. Consider registering your copyrighted work. You can register for a modest fee. Registration serves as unambiguous documentation that your product was in existence at the date of copyright. If you ever get into a legal tussle over ownership, registration can be a huge help.
6. Look for other means of protecting your intellectual property. Although many things are not covered by copyright, they can be protected by other means, usually through trademarks and patents.

Chapter 3 – Frequently Asked Questions (FAQs) on Copyright Law

This is section is dedicated to authors and writers of written content. It answers just about any questions authors and writers might have regarding copyright laws.

Copyright in General

http://www.copyright.gov/help/faq/faq-general.html

What is copyright?
Copyright is a form of protection grounded in the U.S. Constitution and granted by law for original works of authorship fixed in a tangible medium of expression. Copyright covers both published and unpublished works.

What does copyright protect?
Copyright, a form of intellectual property law protects original works of authorship including literary, dramatic, musical, and artistic works, such as poetry, novels, movies, songs, computer software, and architecture. Copyright does not protect facts, ideas, systems, or methods of operation, although it may protect the way these things are expressed. See Circular 1, *Copyright Basics*, section "What Works Are Protected."

How is a copyright different from a patent or a trademark?
Copyright protects original works of authorship, while a patent protects inventions or discoveries. Ideas and discoveries are not protected by the copyright law, although the way in which they are expressed may be. A trademark protects words, phrases, symbols, or designs identifying the source of the goods or services of one party and distinguishing them from those of others.

When is my work protected?
Your work is under copyright protection the moment it is created and fixed in a tangible form that it is perceptible either directly or with the aid of a machine or device.

Do I have to register with your office to be protected?
No. In general, registration is voluntary. Copyright exists from the moment the work is created. You will have to register, however, if you wish to bring a lawsuit for infringement of a U.S. work. See Circular 1, *Copyright Basics*, section "Copyright Registration."

Why should I register my work if copyright protection is automatic?
Registration is recommended for a number of reasons. Many choose to register their works because they wish to have the facts of their copyright on the public record and have a certificate of registration. Registered works may be eligible for statutory damages and attorney's fees in successful litigation. Finally, if registration occurs within 5 years of publication, it is considered *prima facie* evidence in a court of law. See Circular 1, *Copyright Basics*, section "Copyright Registration" and Circular 38b, *Highlights of Copyright Amendments Contained in the Uruguay Round Agreements Act (URAA)*, on non-U.S. works.

I've heard about a "poor man's copyright." What is it?
The practice of sending a copy of your own work to yourself is sometimes called a "poor man's copyright." There is no provision in the copyright law regarding any such type of

protection, and it is not a substitute for registration.

Is my copyright good in other countries?
The United States has copyright relations with most countries throughout the world, and as a result of these agreements, we honor each other's citizens' copyrights. However, the United States does not have such copyright relationships with every country. For a listing of countries and the nature of their copyright relations with the United States, see Circular 38a, *International Copyright Relations of the United States*.

Frequently Asked Questions about Copyright
The Copyright Office offers introductory answers to frequently asked questions about copyright, registration, and services of the Office. Click on a subject heading below to view questions and answers relating to your selection. Links throughout the answers will guide you to further information on our website or from other sources.

Go here to access this page and the hyperlinks offered below:

http://www.copyright.gov/help/faq/

Copyright in General
- What is copyright?
- What does copyright protect?
- How is a copyright different from a patent or a trademark?
- When is my work protected?
- Do I have to register with your office to be protected?
- Why should I register my work if copyright protection is automatic?
- I've heard about a "poor man's copyright." What is it?
- Is my copyright good in other countries?

What Does Copyright Protect?
- What does copyright protect?
- Can I copyright my website?

- Can I copyright my domain name?
- How do I protect my recipe?
- Can I copyright the name of my band?
- How do I copyright a name, title, slogan or logo?
- How do I protect my idea?
- Does my work have to be published to be protected?
- Can I register a diary I found in my grandmother's attic?
- How do I protect my sighting of Elvis?
- Does copyright protect architecture?
- Can I get a star named after me and claim copyright to it?

Who Can Register?
- Can foreigners register their works in the United States?
- Can a minor claim copyright?
- Can I register a diary I found in my grandmother's attic?

Registering a Work
- How do I register my copyright?
- Where can I get application forms?
- Can I make copies of the application form?
- Can I file online?
- What is the registration fee?
- Do you take credit cards?
- Do I have to send in my work? Do I get it back?
- Will my deposit be damaged by security measures in place on Capito
- May I register more than one work on the same application? Where c
- Do I have to use my real name on the form? Can I use a stage name
- Will my personal information be available to the public?
- How long does the registration process take?
- Can I submit my manuscript on a computer disk?
- Can I submit a CD-ROM of my work?
- Does my work have to be published to be protected?
- How much do I have to change in my own work to make a new claim
- Do you have special mailing requirements?

Privacy
- Can I see my copyright registration records?
- Will my registration records help provide contact information for some

my work?
- Can I remove information that I don't want publicized?
- How can I prevent personal information from being placed on the Cc
- Why is my copyright registration information now appearing on searc
Google?

Preregistration
- What is preregistration? What works can be preregistered?
- What classes of works are eligible for preregistration?
- Is preregistration a substitute for registration?
- Will I need to make a regular registration after my work is completed
- When should I register my work if I have already preregistered it?
- How do I preregister?
- What is the effective date of my preregistration?
- How do I complete a preregistration application?
- You ask for a description in the preregistration application. What shc
- Will I receive a certificate for my preregistration?
- What is the fee for preregistration?
- What methods of payment are accepted for preregistration?
- What does ACH (payment) mean?
- Do I receive a password from the Copyright Office to log into the eC
my work? Or do I create my own password?
- What are the password requirements that I should follow when I cre
- How do I change my password?
- What do I do if I forgot my password?

Which Form Should I Use?
- Which form should I use?
- I want to copyright my business name. Which form do I use?
- Which form do I use to register an automated database?
- Which form do I use to register a computer software application I am
- ...is there a form to submit to change the address on my application

I've Submitted My Application, Fee, and Copy of My Work to the What?
- How can I know when my submission for registration is received by
- How long does the registration process take, and when will I receive
- I've been getting solicitation letters from publishers. Is the Copyright

personal...

How Long Does Copyright Protection Last?

- How long does a copyright last?
- Do I have to renew my copyright?

Can I Use Someone Else's Work? Can Someone Else Use Mine?

- How do I get permission to use somebody else's work?
- How can I find out who owns a copyright?
- I found someone infringing a copyrighted work that I registered. Can
me stop this?
- How can I obtain copies of someone else's work and/or registration c
- How much of someone else's work can I use without getting permissi
- How much do I have to change in order to claim copyright in someon
- Somebody infringed my copyright. What can I do?
- Could I be sued for using somebody else's work? How about quotes
- Do you have a list of songs or movies in the public domain?
- I saw an image on the Library of Congress website that I would like t
- Is it legal to download works from peer-to-peer networks and if not, w
- Can a school show a movie without obtaining permission from the co
- My local copying store will not make reproductions of old family phot

Assignment/Transfer of Copyright Ownership

- Are copyrights transferable?
- Do you have any forms for transfer of copyrights?

Copyright and Digital Files

- Can I backup my computer software?
- Can I buy or sell backup copies of computer software?...
- Can I copyright my website?
- Can I copyright my domain name?
- Is it legal to download works from peer-to-peer networks and if not, w

Information about the Copyright Office

- What is your telephone number?
- What is your mailing address?
- What is your street address?
- What are your hours of operation?
- How do I get on your mailing or email list?

Services of the Copyright Office

- Are you the only place I can go to register a copyright?
- Can you provide me with copies of my application and my work?
- I lost my certificate. Can I get a new one?
- Can you tell me who owns a copyright?
- Is the Copyright Office open to the public?
- Does the Copyright Office give legal advice?
- How do I get my work published?
- How do I collect royalties?
- How do I get my work into the Library of Congress

Mandatory Deposit

- What is mandatory deposit?
- We are a foreign publisher. Do we need to submit our publication to
- What is the difference between mandatory deposit and copyright reg
- Where do I send my published works to comply with mandatory dep
- If I choose to register my copyright, should I use the same address t
- Is there an exception to mandatory deposits?
- If my publication does not have a copyright notice, do I still have to d
- What is the difference between the mandatory deposit obligation and
- Will my Cataloging In Publication (CIP) copy fulfill my mandatory dep
- If I send deposit copies of a sample issue of my serial publication to Copyrights...
- I have already deposited identifying material to register my compute

Newspapers on Microfilm

- Do I still need to submit a copy of the 35mm silver positive to apply f registration...
- Can we still register our copyright with the Copyright Office if the Lib not...
- What are the requirements for applying for the newspaper group reg
- How do I register my daily newspaper through group registration?
- Since copyright protection exists when the work is created, is it nece

Definitions

- Who is an author?
- What is a deposit?
- What is publication?

- What is a copyright notice? How do I put a copyright notice on my wo
- What is copyright infringement?
- What is peer-to-peer (P2P) networking?
- Where is the public domain?
- What is mandatory deposit?
- What is a work made for hire?
- What is a Library of Congress number?
- What is an ISBN number?
- What are some other commonly used terms?

Special Handling FAQs

- What is special handling
- When is special handling granted?
- How long does it take to process special handling cases?
- What's the best way to expedite processing?
- How much does it cost for special handling?

In the section below, it is important to learn when and how you can use other author's works. This is an important section so study the information carefully.

Can I Use Someone Else's Work? Can Someone Else Use Mine?

http://www.copyright.gov/help/faq/faq-fairuse.html

How do I get permission to use somebody else's work?
You can ask for it. If you know who the copyright owner is, you may contact the owner directly. If you are not certain about the ownership or have other related questions, you may wish to request that the Copyright Office conduct a search of its records or you may search yourself. See the next question for more details.

How can I find out who owns a copyright?
We can provide you with the information available in our records. A search of registrations, renewals, and recorded transfers of ownership made before 1978 requires a manual

search of our files. Upon request, our staff will search our records at the statutory rate of $165 for each hour (2 hour minimum). There is no fee if you conduct a search in person at the Copyright Office. Copyright registrations made and documents recorded from 1978 to date are available for searching online. For further information, see Circular 22, *How to Investigate the Copyright Status of a Work*, and Circular 23, *Copyright Card Catalog and the Online File*.

How can I obtain copies of someone else's work and/or registration certificate?

The Copyright Office will not honor a request for a copy of someone else's protected work without written authorization from the copyright owner or from his or her designated agent, unless the work is involved in litigation. In the latter case, a litigation statement is required. A certificate of registration for any registered work can be obtained for a fee of $35. Circular 6, *Access to and Copies of Copyright Records and Deposit*, provides additional information.

How much of someone else's work can I use without getting permission?

Under the *fair use* doctrine of the U.S. copyright statute, it is permissible to use limited portions of a work including quotes, for purposes such as commentary, criticism, news reporting, and scholarly reports. There are no legal rules permitting the use of a specific number of words, a certain number of musical notes, or percentage of a work. Whether a particular use qualifies as fair use depends on all the circumstances. See FL 102, Fair Use, and Circular 21, *Reproductions of Copyrighted Works by Educators and Librarians*.

How much do I have to change in order to claim copyright in someone else's work?

Only the owner of copyright in a work has the right to prepare, or to authorize someone else to create, a new version of that work. Accordingly, you cannot claim copyright to another's work, no matter how much you change it, unless you have the owner's consent. See Circular 14, *Copyright Registration for Derivative Works*.

Somebody infringed my copyright. What can I do?
A party may seek to protect his or her copyrights against unauthorized use by filing a civil lawsuit in federal district court. If you believe that your copyright has been infringed, consult an attorney. In cases of willful infringement for profit, the U.S. Attorney may initiate a criminal investigation.

Could I be sued for using somebody else's work? How about quotes or samples?
If you use a copyrighted work without authorization, the owner may be entitled to bring an infringement action against you. There are circumstances under the fair use doctrine where a quote or a sample may be used without permission. However, in cases of doubt, the Copyright Office recommends that permission be obtained.

Do you have a list of songs or movies in the public domain?
No, we neither compile nor maintain such a list. A search of our records, however, may reveal whether a particular work has fallen into the public domain. We will conduct a search of our records by the title of a work, an author's name, or a claimant's name. Upon request, our staff will search our records at the statutory rate of $165 for each hour (2 hour minimum). You may also search the records in person without paying a fee.

I saw an image on the Library of Congress website that I would like to use. Do I need to obtain permission?
With few exceptions, the Library of Congress does not own copyright in the materials in its collections and does not grant or deny permission to use the content mounted on its website. Responsibility for making an independent legal assessment of an item from the Library's collections and for securing any necessary permissions rests with persons desiring to use the item. To the greatest extent possible, the Library attempts to provide any known rights information about its collections. Such information can be found in the "Copyright and Other

Restrictions" statements on each American Memory online collection homepage. If the image is not part of the American Memory collections, contact the Library custodial division to which the image is credited. Bibliographic records and finding aids available in each custodial division include information that may assist in assessing the copyright status. Search our catalogs through the Library's Online Catalog. To access information from the Library's reading rooms, go to Research Centers.

Is it legal to download works from peer-to-peer networks and if not, what is the penalty for doing so?

Uploading or downloading works protected by copyright without the authority of the copyright owner is an infringement of the copyright owner's exclusive rights of reproduction and/or distribution. Anyone found to have infringed a copyrighted work may be liable for statutory damages up to $30,000 for each work infringed and, if willful infringement is proven by the copyright owner, that amount may be increased up to $150,000 for each work infringed. In addition, an infringer of a work may also be liable for the attorney's fees incurred by the copyright owner to enforce his or her rights.

Whether or not a particular work is being made available under the authority of the copyright owner is a question of fact. But since any original work of authorship fixed in a tangible medium (including a computer file) is protected by federal copyright law upon creation, in the absence of clear information to the contrary, most works may be assumed to be protected by federal copyright law.

Since the files distributed over peer-to-peer networks are primarily copyrighted works, there is a risk of liability for downloading material from these networks. To avoid these risks, there are currently many "authorized" services on the Internet that allow consumers to purchase copyrighted works online, whether music, ebooks, or motion pictures. By purchasing works through authorized services, consumers can avoid the risks of infringement liability and can limit their exposure to other potential risks, e.g., viruses, unexpected material, or spyware.

Can a school show a movie without obtaining permission from the copyright owner?
If the movie is for entertainment purposes, you need to get a clearance or license for its performance.

It is not necessary to obtain permission if you show the movie in the course of "face-to-face teaching activities" in a nonprofit educational institution, in a classroom or similar place devoted to instruction, if the copy of the movie being performed is a lawful copy. 17 U.S.C. § 110(1). This exemption encompasses instructional activities relating to a wide variety of subjects, but it does not include performances for recreation or entertainment purposes, even if there is cultural value or intellectual appeal.

Questions regarding this provision of the copyright law should be made to the legal counsel of the school or school system.

My local copying store will not make reproductions of old family photographs. What can I do?
Photocopying shops, photography stores and other photo developing stores are often reluctant to make reproductions of old photographs for fear of violating the copyright law and being sued. These fears are not unreasonable, because copy shops have been sued for reproducing copyrighted works and have been required to pay substantial damages for infringing copyrighted works. The policy established by a shop is a business decision and risk assessment that the business is entitled to make, because the business may face liability if they reproduce a work even if they did not know the work was copyrighted.

In the case of photographs, it is sometimes difficult to determine who owns the copyright and there may be little or no information about the owner on individual copies. Ownership of a "copy" of a photograph – the tangible embodiment of the “work” – is distinct from the “work” itself – the intangible intellectual property. The owner of the “work” is generally the photographer or, in certain situations, the employer of the photographer. Even if a person hires a photographer to take pictures of a wedding, for example, the photographer will own the copyright in the photographs unless the copyright in the photographs is transferred, in writing and signed by the copyright owner, to another person. The subject of the photograph generally has nothing to do with the ownership of the copyright in the photograph. If the photographer is no longer living, the rights in the photograph are determined by the photographer’s will or passed as personal property by the applicable laws of intestate succession.

There may be situations in which the reproduction of a photograph may be a “fair use” under the copyright law. Information about fair use may be found at: www.copyright.gov/fls/fl102.html. However, even if a person determines a use to be a “fair use” under the factors of section 107 of the Copyright Act, a copy shop or other third party need not accept the person’s assertion that the use is noninfringing. Ultimately, only a federal court can determine whether a particular use is, in fact, a fair use under the law.

Chapter 4 – The CENDI Copyright Working Group

Prepared by
CENDI Copyright Working Group

Edited and updated by
Bonnie Klein
Defense Technical and Information Center
and
Gail Hodge
Information International Associates, Inc.

Published by
CENDI Secretariat
Information International Associates, Inc.
Oak Ridge, TN
October 2008

The following is prepared by the CENDO Copyright Working Group and without a doubt is the most comprehensive working paper on the subject of copyrights. Access to the page and hyperlinks can be found here;

http://www.cendi.gov/publications/04-8copyright.html#211

1.0 GLOSSARY OF TERMS

Author, under the U.S. Copyright Law, is either the person who actually creates a copyrightable work or, if the copyrightable work is created within the scope of employment, the employer of the person who actually creates the copyrightable work.

Berne Convention[1] is the Convention for the Protection of Literary and Artistic Works, signed at Berne, Switzerland, on September 9, 1886, and all acts, protocols, and revisions to these documents.

Clearance - see Permission

Collective work is a work, such as a periodical issue, anthology, or encyclopedia, in which a number of contributions, constituting separate and independent works in themselves, are assembled into a collective whole.

Compilation is a work formed by the collection and assembling of preexisting materials or of data that are selected, coordinated, or arranged in such a way that the resulting work as a whole constitutes an original work of authorship. The term "compilation" includes collective works.

Copyright refers to the exclusive rights granted to an author or owner of a copyrightable work. (See FAQ Section 2.1 and 17 USC § 106.[2])

Copyright Management Information (CMI) is defined under the Digital Millennium Copyright Act (DMCA)[3] as identifying information about a work, author, copyright owner, and in certain cases, the performer, writer or director of a work, as well as terms and conditions for use of the work, and such other information as the Register of Copyrights may prescribe by regulation. (See FAQ Section 2.4.6 and 17 USC § 1202(c).[4])

Copyright owner, with respect to any one of the exclusive rights comprised in a copyright, refers to the owner of that particular right. The exclusive rights provided by Copyright are completely divisible. Copyright in a work vests initially in the author or authors of the work. However, the author may assign some or all of his or her rights to another, e.g., to a publisher, if the work has appeared in a formal publication, who then becomes the owner of the rights assigned.

Derivative Work refers to a work that is based on, or modifies, one or more preexisting works. A copyright owner has the exclusive right to prepare or authorize the preparation of a derivative work based on the copyrighted work. If a derivative work, considered as a whole, represents an original work of authorship, it may be separately copyrightable. However, the copyright covers only original portions of the derivative work.

Fair Use is a statutory exception that allows the use of a copyrighted work for certain purposes without requiring permission. (See 17 USC § 107[5]).

Federal Acquisition Regulation (FAR)[6] was established to codify uniform policies for acquisition of supplies and services by executive agencies. It is issued and maintained jointly, pursuant to the OFPP Reauthorization Act, under the statutory authorities granted to the Secretary of Defense (DoD), Administrator of General Services (GSA) and the Administrator, National Aeronautics and Space Administration (NASA). The official FAR appears in the Code of Federal Regulations at 48 CFR Chapter 1.

First Sale Doctrine refers to the right of a buyer of a material object in which a copyrighted work is embodied to resell or transfer the object itself. Ownership of copyright is distinct from ownership of the material object. Section 109 of the Copyright Act permits the owner of a particular copy or phonorecord lawfully made under the Copyright Law to sell or otherwise dispose of possession of that copy or phonorecord without the authority of the copyright owner. Commonly referred to as the "first sale doctrine," this provision permits such activities as the sale of used books. The first sale doctrine is subject to limitations that permit a copyright owner to prevent the unauthorized commercial rental of computer programs and sound recordings. (See 17 USC § 202[7] and 17 USC § 109[8].)

Government Distribution or Dissemination means, in accordance with OMB Circular A-130,[9] Management of Federal Information Resources, the Government initiated distribution of information to the public. Dissemination within the meaning of the Circular does not include distribution limited to government employees or agency contractors or grantees, intra- or inter-agency use or sharing of government information, and responses to requests for agency records under the Freedom of Information Act (FOIA) (5 U.S.C. § 552[10]) or Privacy Act[11].

Government Publication is informational matter that is published as an individual document at Government expense or as required by law. (See Title 44 USC § 1901[12])

Government Records are all books, papers, maps, photographs, machine-readable materials, or other documentary materials, regardless of physical form or characteristics, made or received by an agency of the United States Government under federal law or in connection with the transaction of public business and preserved or appropriate for preservation by that agency or its legitimate successor as evidence of the organization, functions, policies, decisions, procedures, operations, or other activities of the Government or because of the informational value of the data in them. Library and museum material made or acquired and preserved solely for reference or exhibition purposes, extra copies of documents preserved only for convenience of reference, and stocks of publications and of processed documents are not included. (See 44 USC § 3301[13])

U.S. Government Work or a "work of the United States Government" is a work prepared by an officer or employee of the United States Government as part of that person's official duties. (See 17 USC § 101. Definitions.[14]) In these FAQ's, the term "U.S. Government work" will be used to refer to a work of the United States Government and is distinct from works of state governments. (See FAQ Section 3.1.3).

Intellectual Property refers to intangible property rights such as copyright, patents and trademarks that provide the owner with certain exclusive rights.

Joint Work is a work prepared by two or more authors with the intention that their contributions be merged into inseparable or interdependent parts of a unitary whole. (See 17 USC § 101. Definitions.[15]) The authors of a joint work are co-owners of copyright in the work. (See 17 USC § 201(a).[16])

License is a contractual agreement from a copyright owner or the owner's authorized agent, such as a third party vendor, allowing another party to exercise one or more of the exclusive rights provided the copyright owner under the Copyright Law (See FAQ Section 2.1.5). Licenses usually involve the payment of a fee or royalty. However, royalty free licenses are also legally possible; for example, see the National Library of Medicine *License Agreement for Use of the UMLS® Metathesaurus®*.[17]

Permission is an agreement from a copyright owner allowing another party to exercise one or more of the exclusive rights provided the copyright owner under the Copyright Law (See FAQ Section 2.1.5. Permission generally does not involve the transfer of any fees or reimbursements. Permission may also be referred to as a Copyright Release.

Publication is the distribution of copies or phonorecords of a work to the public by sale or other transfer of ownership or by rental, lease, or lending. The offering to distribute copies or phonorecords to a group of persons for purposes of further distribution, public performance, or public display, constitutes publication. A public performance or display of a work does not of itself constitute publication. (See 17 USC § 101. Definitions.[18])

Transfer of copyright ownership is the act of transferring any or all of the exclusive rights comprised in a copyright from the copyright owner to another person or institution.

Ownership is generally transferred through an assignment, mortgage, or exclusive license, whether or not it is limited in time or place of effect, but not including a nonexclusive license. (See 17 USC § 201(d)(2).[19]) Transfers must be in writing and must be signed by the party making the transfer. (See 17 USC § 204.[20])

2.0 COPYRIGHT BASICS

2.1 General Information Regarding Copyright

2.1.1 What is copyright?

Copyright is a form of protection provided by the laws of the United States (Title 17 of the United States Code (17 USC - Copyrights)[21]) to the authors of original works of authorship including literary, dramatic, musical, artistic, and certain other intellectual works. (See also Title 37 Code of Federal Regulations (37 CFR, Chapter II)[22], which implements this statute.) Copyright protection arises automatically once an original work of authorship is fixed in a tangible medium of expression, now known or later developed; e.g., written, filmed, recorded. It does not require that a copyright notice be placed on the work, that the work be published, or that the work be deposited or registered with the Copyright Office or any other body.

2.1.2 What is the history of copyright legislation in the U.S.?

The basis for Copyright Law comes from the U.S. Constitution, Article 1, Section 8.[23]

"The Congress shall have power... to promote the Progress of Science and useful Arts, by securing for limited times to Authors and Inventors the exclusive right to their respective Writings and Discoveries."

The first federal Copyright Act enacted in 1790 was a codification of longstanding judicial doctrine. Since that date, Congress has periodically enacted major copyright revision bills modernizing the statute. The last copyright revision bill was enacted in 1976.

While most of the provisions of the current Copyright Law were contained in the Copyright Act of 1976, on a number of occasions Congress has amended that legislation to address new concerns. For example, in 1988 a number of changes were embraced to permit United States accession to the Berne Convention[24]. More recently, the copyright term was increased by the Sonny Bono Copyright Term Extension Act,[25] and issues relating to digital works were addressed in the Digital Millennium Copyright Act.[26] (See FAQ Section 2.4.6).

2.1.3 What works are eligible for copyright protection?

Copyright requires an original work of authorship to be fixed in a tangible medium of expression from which it can be perceived either directly or with the aid of a machine or device. Copyright protects the form of expression only and does not extend to the idea or concept underlying the work. (See FAQ Section 2.5, Other Forms of Intellectual Property Protection, for a discussion of the differences between copyright and other forms of intellectual property protection such as patents and trademarks.)

Categories of copyrightable works under Title 17 USC § 201 include: literary works such as educational materials and computer programs; musical works, including any accompanying words; dramatic works, including any accompanying music; pictorial, graphic and sculptural works; motion pictures and other audiovisual works; sound recordings; and architectural works. For U.S. Government works, see FAQ Section 3.

2.1.4 Can facts, databases and compilations be copyrighted?

Facts cannot be copyrighted. However, the creative selection, coordination and arrangement of information and materials forming a database or compilation may be protected by copyright. Note, however, that the copyright protection only extends to the creative aspect, not to the facts contained in the database or compilation.

2.1.5 What rights does copyright provide?

As stated in 17 USC § 106[27], copyright gives the owner of the copyright the exclusive right to do and to authorize others to do the following:

- To reproduce the copyrighted work in copies or phonorecords;
- To prepare derivative works based upon the copyrighted work;
- To distribute copies or phonorecords of the copyrighted work to the public by sale or other transfer of ownership, or by rental, lease, or lending;
- To perform the copyrighted work publicly, in the case of literary, musical, dramatic, and choreographic works, pantomimes, motion pictures and other audiovisual works;
- To display the copyrighted work publicly, in the case of literary, musical, dramatic, and choreographic works, pantomimes, and pictorial, graphic, or sculptural works, including the individual images of a motion picture or other audiovisual work; and
- In the case of sound recordings, to perform the work publicly by means of a digital audio transmission.

In addition, certain authors of works of visual art have the rights of attribution and integrity described in 17 USC § 106A[28]. Limitations are outlined in FAQ Section 2.2.1.

For further discussion, see U.S. Copyright Office, Circular 101: Copyright Basics,[29] and Circular 40, Copyright Registration for Works of the Visual Arts.[30]

2.1.6 How long does copyright last?

Under current Copyright Law, the copyright term for works created by individuals on or after January 1, 1978, is the life of the author plus 70 years. For "works made for hire," the copyright term is 95 years from the date of first publication or 120 years from the date of its creation, whichever is earliest. The copyright term for works created before January 1, 1978, is a complicated determination and may require help from your General Counsel or the Copyright Office.

The current Copyright Law established dates at which Copyright protection for unpublished works expires and those works pass into the public domain. Unpublished works created prior to January 1, 1978, and not published, will pass into the public domain 70 years after the author's death or at the end of 2002, whichever is later. Unpublished works created prior to January 1, 1978, but which are published between then and the end of 2002, will pass into the public domain 70 years after the author's death or at the end of 2047, whichever is later.

Additionally, all works published before 1923 are now in the public domain.

Publications that may help in this determination include:

The U.S. Copyright Law, Chapter 3 -- Duration of Copyright[31]

Information Circular 15a - Duration of Copyright: Provisions of the Law Dealing with the Length of Copyright Protection [32]

Fact sheet FL 15 - New Terms for Copyright Protection[33]

When Works Pass Into the Public Domain[34]

2.1.7 Is the copyright term extended or changed merely by copying the work to another medium; e.g., from print to CD-ROM?

No, the term of protection of a work is not affected by the fact that the owner has copied the work to another medium. If, in addition, new information is added, the new information if copyrightable could have its own term of protection.

2.2 Limitation on Copyright Protection

2.2.1 Are there any limitations to copyright protection?

Yes, 17 USC §§ 107 through 120[35] establish limitations or exceptions on these exclusive rights. One limitation is the doctrine of "fair use," which is set forth in 17 USC § 107[36]. (See FAQ Section 2.2.2 on Fair Use.) Other limitations include provisions for allowing compulsory licenses, use and copying by libraries, the sale of the work by the owner (See FAQ Section 1.0, Glossary, for definition of the "First Sale Doctrine") and uses which fall outside of the enumerated exclusive rights, such as performances that are not public.

2.2.2 What is "fair use"?

A fair use of a copyrighted work may include the practice of any of the exclusive rights provided by copyright, for example, reproduction for purposes such as criticism comment, news reporting, teaching (including multiple copies for classroom use), scholarship, or research. The "fair use" limitation found at 17 USC § 107,[37] is not defined in the statute and does not provide a bright line rule for determining what is or is not a fair use. Rather it identifies four factors that should be evaluated on a case-by-case basis in order to determine if a specific use is "fair". These factors, which should be considered together when determining fair use, are:

1. Purpose and character of the use, including whether such use is of a commercial nature or is for nonprofit educational purposes;
2. Nature of the copyrighted work;
3. Amount and substantiality of the portion used in relation to the copyrighted work as a whole; and
4. Effect of the use upon the potential market for or value of the copyrighted work.

The distinction between "fair use" and infringement can be unclear and is not easily defined. There is no right number of words, lines or notes that qualify as a fair use.

2.2.3 May the U.S. Government use the fair use exception?

Yes, the "fair use" exception applies to the U.S. Government. As with any other user, the use of copyrighted information by Government agencies and employees is assessed by the fair use factors to determine if the use is "fair" under 17 USC § 107. (See FAQ Section 5.1.1)

2.2.4 What is public domain?

Public domain refers to works that are not protected by copyright and are publicly available. They may be used by anyone, anywhere, anytime without permission, license or royalty payment.

A work may enter the public domain because the term of copyright protection has expired (see FAQ Section 2.1.6), because copyright has been abandoned, or in the U.S. because it is a U.S. Government work and there is no other statutory basis for the Government to restrict its access (see FAQ Section 3.1.5).

A work is not in the public domain simply because it does not have a copyright notice. Additionally, the fact that a privately created work is, with permission, included in a U.S.

Government work does not place the private work into the public domain. The user is responsible for determining whether a work is in the public domain.

It is important to read the permissions and copyright notices on U.S. Government publications and Web sites. Many Government agencies follow the practice of providing notice for material that is copyrighted and not for those that are in the public domain. Examples of government agency copyright policies and statements are: National Library of Medicine,[38] NASA Center for AeroSpace Information (CASI),[39] and Library of Congress.[40]

2.2.5 Can a work that includes works in the public domain be copyrighted?

Yes. However, the copyright protects only the original contributions added by the author.

2.2.6 Does public release, disclosure or dissemination mean the same as public domain?

No, these terms are not synonymous and should not be used interchangeably. Public release, disclosure and dissemination describe the availability of a work. Publicly released, disclosed or disseminated information may be owned and protected by copyright, and therefore, not be in the public domain.

2.3 Ownership of Copyright

2.3.1 Who can hold copyright?

Copyright ownership may be held by any person or institution. Typically, the author of a work owns the copyright in the work. However, under the U.S. Copyright Law, for a work made for hire, that is a work prepared by an employee within the scope of employment or a specially ordered or commissioned work, the employer or other person for whom the work was prepared is considered the author.

2.3.2 Can copyright be transferred from the author or owner to another party?

Yes, any and all of the copyright owner's exclusive rights may be transferred, but the transfer of exclusive rights is not valid unless that transfer is in writing and signed by the owner of the rights being transferred. (See 17 USC § 204.[41]) Transfer of a right on a nonexclusive basis does not require a written agreement; however, you should check your Agency's policy.

No effective transfer of copyright can be made in the U.S. for U.S. Government works (see FAQ Section 3.0), because they are not eligible for copyright protection under the U.S. Copyright Law.

2.3.3 How can the owner of a copyrighted work be identified?

If you want to contact the copyright owner regarding use of a copyrighted work, the best place to start is with the work itself. Copyright notices in published works identify the owner at the time the work was published. However, copyright ownership may have changed since publication. The copyright notice and any permissions are often printed on the back of the title page in books. Most owners will be apparent, particularly for relatively current works. However, identifying the specific owner may be more difficult for journal articles, gray literature and older works. Affiliation of the author may suggest ownership or may help to locate the individual author, but is not in itself definitive. The U.S. Copyright Office provides some suggestions in Copyright Office Circular 22.[42]

Additionally, Copyright Office records, including registration information and recorded documents, are available through LOCIS (Library of Congress Information System[43]), or a newer web-based search system. Information, including ownership information, is available for works registered for copyright since January 1, 1978. The information may be searched online by title of the work, author and copyright claimant.

2.4 Copyright and the Internet

2.4.1 Does the Copyright Law apply to materials on the Internet or the Web?

Yes, the Internet is another form of publishing or disseminating information; therefore, copyright applies to Web sites, e-mail messages, Web-based music, etc. Simply because the Internet provides easy access to the information does not mean that the information is in the public domain or is available without limitations. Copyrighted works found on the Internet should be treated the same as copyrighted works found in other media.

2.4.2 Can the published version of a U.S. Government work that has been published in a non-government product be posted on a public Web site?

It depends. If the publisher has made original and creative contributions to the published work, the publisher may have some rights. Check with your General Counsel's Office or agency policy. Alternatively, the original manuscript as submitted to the publisher could be posted. (See FAQ Sections 3.2.3 and 3.2.4.)

2.4.3 Does fair use apply to the Internet?

Yes, fair use applies to materials and use of works found or placed on the Internet. The same factors will be considered as for fair use in print (see FAQ Section 2.2.2).

2.4.4 How can I determine what uses can be made of materials found on the Internet?

As in the print environment, it is not necessary for an author to include a copyright statement on the material in order for the work to maintain its copyright protection. However, you may find notices on the home page or on special terms and condition pages that provide for specific uses.

2.4.5 Are copyright notices required on materials on Government Web sites?

It is good practice to provide notice whenever possible, even though it is not required. In addition, there may be disclaimers and use notices that apply to use of the material. Check your Agency policy regarding Web site notices. For further discussion, see the CENDI Whitepaper, *Don't Keep the Public Guessing: Best Practices in Notice of Copyright and Terms & Conditions of Use for Government Website Content (CENDI/04-4)*. Also see examples listed in Section 6.0.

2.4.6. Is it a copyright infringement to link from your website to copyrighted material on another?

No. In April, 2000, Federal Judge Harry L. Hupp in his ruling on deep linking in Ticketmaster vs. Tickets.com, Inc., 2000 U.S. Dist. LEXIS 12987 (D. Cal. 2000) states that, "...hyperlinking does not itself involve a violation of the Copyright Act (whatever it may do for other claims) since no copying is involved." Many organizations encourage links by posting terms and conditions and how-to instructions on their websites, usually under the headings of Copyright, Legal Notices, or About Us. For examples, see the *Washington Post*[44]and the *New York Times*[45]. However, be aware of "other claims" and court rulings which prohibit framing, misuse of trademarks, bypassing advertising, etc.

2.4.7 Does the Digital Millennium Copyright Act (DMCA) of 1998 expand protection of works on the Internet?

Yes, the DMCA (Pub. L. No. 105-304, 112 Stat. 2860[46]) added Chapter 12 to the U.S. Copyright Law[47]. The DMCA prohibits any person from circumventing a technological measure that effectively controls access to a work protected under the U.S.

Copyright Act, 17 U.S.C. § 1201(a)(1)[48]. The Copyright Office will determine whether any classes of works should be subject to exemptions for the prohibitions and will publish lists of such exempt classes. The DMCA also makes it illegal for a person to manufacture, import, offer to the public, provide or otherwise traffic in any technology, product, service, device, component or part thereof which is primarily designed or produced to circumvent a technological measure that effectively controls access to or unauthorized copying of a work protected by copyright, has only a limited commercially significant purpose or use other than circumvention of such measures, or is marketed for use in circumventing such measures, 17 U.S.C. § 1201(a)(2)[49].

In addition the DMCA prohibits, among other actions, the intentional removal or alteration of copyright management information and the knowing addition of false copyright management information if these acts are done with intent to induce, enable, facilitate or conceal a copyright infringement, 17 U.S.C. § 1202[50]. Each prohibition is subject to a number of statutory exceptions.

The DMCA also provides certain limitations on service provider liability with respect to information residing, at direction of a user, on a system or network that the service provider controls or operates, 17 U.S.C. § 512[51]. However, this "safe harbor" provision may not be necessary for Government agencies qualifying as service providers because they are not liable for contributory copyright infringement (see FAQ Section 5.1.1).

Further, the DMCA creates an exemption for making a copy of a computer program by activating a computer for purposes of maintenance or repair. For further discussion, see the U.S. Copyright Office Summary of the DMCA[52].

2.5 Other Forms of Intellectual Property Protection

2.5.1 Are there other forms of intellectual property protection?

Yes, there are other forms of intellectual property protection including patents and trademarks. Copyright differs from patents and trademarks in both the terms and kind of coverage that is granted. Copyright protects original works of authorship such as literary works, phonorecords, dramatic works, etc. Patents[53] protect new, useful and non-obvious inventions such as processes, machines, manufactures and compositions of matter. Trademarks[54] protect words, phrases, symbols or designs, such as logos or names of products or organizations that identify and distinguish the source of goods or services of one party from those of another. Each type of intellectual property differs in the subject matter and requirements for protection, the length of time that the protection holds, how it can be transferred, the basis and penalties incurred for infringement of the exclusive rights provided, and the kind of exemptions that are allowed. For more information, contact the U.S. Patent and Trademark Office.[55]

3.0 U.S. GOVERNMENT WORKS

3.1 Government Works

3.1.1 What is a U.S. Government work?

A "work of the United States Government," referred to in this document as a U.S. Government work, is a work prepared by an officer or employee of the United States Government as part of that person's official duties. (See 17 USC § 101, Definitions.[56])

Contractors, grantees and certain categories of people who work with the government are not considered government employees for purposes of copyright. Also not all government publications and government records are government works (See FAQ Section 1.0, Definitions).

An officer's or employee's official duties are the duties assigned to the individual as a result of employment. Generally, official duties would be described in a position description and include other incidental duties. Official duties do not include work done at a government officer's or employee's own volition, even if the subject matter is government work, so long as the work was not required as part of the individual's official duty. (S.REP. NO. 473, 94th Cong., 2d Sess. 56-57) (1976) "A government official or employee should not be prevented from securing copyright in a work written at his own volition and outside his duties, even though the subject matter involves his government work or his professional field.") For further discussion, see Tresansky, John O. Copyright in Government Employee Authored Works. [57] 30 Cath. L. Rev. 605 (1981).

The following cases give examples of some related issues:

Public Affairs Associates v. Rickover [58] 284 F.2d 262, 268 n.20 (D.C. Cir. 1960), vacated on other grounds for insufficient record, 369 U.S. 111 (1962)

Herbert. v. United States, 36 Fed. Cl. 299 (Fed. Cl. 1996). The court said: "The specific task need not be individually assigned in order to qualify as part of the official functions of a government employee. Where a government employee's official functions include research, generally, the employee may lose the right to sue for copyright infringement even where he was not specifically required to perform the work at issue."

3.1.2 Is a U.S. Government work provided copyright protection?

In the United States, U.S. Government works are covered by 17 USC § 105.[59] "Copyright protection ... is not available for any work of the United States Government, but the United States is not precluded from receiving and holding copyrights transferred to it by assignment, bequest, or otherwise."

Exceptions are available for certain works of the National Institute for Standards and Technology (NIST) and the U.S. Postal Service. Copyright protection may be available for U.S. Government works outside the United States (see FAQ Section 3.1.6). When a copyrighted work is transferred to the U.S. Government, the Government becomes the copyright owner and the work retains its copyright protection.

3.1.3 Does 17 USC §105[60] apply to works of State and Local Governments?

No, it applies only to federal government works. State and local governments may and often do claim copyright in their publications. It is their prerogative to set policies that may allow, require, restrict or prohibit claim of copyright on some or all works produced by their government units.

3.1.4 What is the history of the copyright treatment of U.S. Government works?

Ever since 1895, statutory provisions have prohibited the assertion of copyright in any publication of the U.S. Government. The provisions have been only slightly modified since their enactment. See "Copyright in Government Publications: Historical Background, Judicial Interpretation, and Legislative Clarification." CPT Brian R. Price. Military Law Review. Vol. 74. (1976), p. 19-63.

3.1.5 Since U.S. Government works are not protected by copyright in the U.S., are all U.S. Government works publicly available without restriction in the U.S.?

No. The fact that U.S. Government works are not protected under the U.S. Copyright Law does not create a requirement that all U.S. Government works be made publicly available without restriction (See Gellman, Robert M. Twin Evils: Government Copyright and Copyright-like Controls Over Government Information. Syracuse Law Review, 999, 1995.

ADA394923 [61]). See Pfeiffer v. Central Intelligence Agency [62], 60 F.3d 861 (D.C. Cir. 1995). Federal laws and agency policies govern the public release of U.S. Government information. Examples include Executive Order 13292, Classified National Security Information , OMB Circular A-130,[63] Management of Federal Information Resources, Department of Defense Directive 5230.9 Clearance of DoD Information for Public Release, April 9, 1996, ASD (PA)[64] and DOD Instruction 5230.29 Security and Policy Review of DoD Information for Public Release.[65] However, while the Government is not required to publicly disseminate all U.S. Government works, the Government does not restrict the use or distribution of most categories of U.S. Government works.

Despite the general policy of free and open information dissemination, there are exceptions based on a number of factors. Certain statutes (see Freedom of Information Act (FOIA) Exemptions)[66] provide the Government with authority to restrict access to U.S. Government works, for example, for purposes of national security, export control, and the filing of patent applications. U.S. Government works should undergo appropriate security, export control and policy reviews by the releasing agency before being cleared for public availability. Additionally, for the purposes of specific agreements, such as Cooperative Research and Development Agreements (CRADA's[67]) and NASA Space Act Agreements[68], the Government has statutory authority to withhold from public dissemination, including dissemination under FOIA, certain Government produced information for a specified period of time.

Some agencies may have additional statutory authority to impose conditions for use. Reasons include ensuring that copyrighted information contained in the government product is recognized, adhering to agreements with other parties, and maintaining contact with users to ensure maintenance and updating of critical information. For example, see NLM's Terms and Conditions for the Visible Human Project[69] and the License Agreement for Use of the UMLS® Metathesaurus®.[70]

Issues related to joint authorship or sponsorship with non-government authors or organizations may also arise.

3.1.6 If an item has a GPO number (#) or an Agency number (#), can I assume it is not copyrighted?

No, not all Government Printing Office or Government agency publications are U.S. Government works. For example, Government Printing Office publications and Agency publications may include works copyrighted by a contractor or grantee; copyrighted material assigned to the U.S. Government; or copyrighted information from other sources.

3.1.7 Does the Government have copyright protection in U.S. Government works in other countries?

Yes, the copyright exclusion for works of the U.S. Government is not intended to have any impact on protection of these works abroad (S. REP. NO. 473, 94th Cong., 2d Sess. 56 (1976)). Therefore, the U.S. Government may obtain protection in other countries depending on the treatment of government works by the national copyright law of the particular country. Copyright is sometimes asserted by U.S. Government agencies outside the United States.

3.1.8 Is the Government required to provide notice that there is no U.S. copyright on its works?

No, but while such a notice is not required, it is helpful to potential users of the material to identify any rights the Government may or may not have in the work. Agencies may have policies about providing notice. For more information, consult your General Counsel.

A good example of a notice is:

This is a work of the U.S. Government and is not subject to copyright protection in the United States. Foreign copyrights may apply.

To avoid confusion in situations where Government works are included in compilations with non-government material, the Government should put notices on every copyrighted item included in a U.S. Government work. Documentation related to permissions granted to the Government for use of such works should be retained.

3.1.9 Are Government websites provided copyright protection?

In accordance with 17 USC §105[71], works prepared by government employees as part of their official duties are not subject to copyright protection in the U.S. (See FAQ Sections 3.1.1 and 3.1.2). This applies to government employee prepared works posted to government Web sites and to the government website itself if government employees as part of their official duties prepare it.

However, if a government web site is developed or maintained by a contractor, parts of the web site authored by the contractor that are subject to copyright protection (i.e., that qualify as copyrightable subject matter) are protected by copyright. Ownership of the copyright and the respective rights of the Government and the contractor are in accordance with the terms of the contract under which the web site was developed or maintained. Additionally, it is possible that copyrighted works owned by others may be posted to government web sites. Copyrighted works that are not owned by the Government should be included on government web sites only with permission of the copyright owner and should include an appropriate copyright notice.

3.2 Government Works Included In Non-Government Works

3.2.1 May another publisher or individual republish a U.S. Government work and assert copyright?

A publisher or individual can republish a U.S. Government work, but the publisher or individual cannot legally assert copyright unless the publisher or individual has added original, copyright protected material. In such a case, copyright protection extends only to the original material that has been added by the publisher or individual. (See 17 USC § 403[72] regarding copyright notice requirements for works incorporating U.S. Government works.)

3.2.2 Can a U.S. Government work be copyrighted if it is included in conference proceedings with other works that are copyrighted?

No, a U.S. Government work is not protected by copyright in the U.S (see FAQ Section 3.1.2). However, other works in the proceedings may be copyrighted (see FAQ Section 2.1.4). Additionally, the creative aspect of the compilation of materials, e.g., selection, coordination or arrangement, may be protected by copyright.

3.2.3 May the Government reproduce and disseminate U.S. Government works, such as journal articles or conference papers, which have been first published or disseminated by the private sector?

Assuming the article is written by a government employee as part of his or her official duties and the publisher does not add original, copyright protected content, then the government may reproduce and disseminate an exact copy of the published work either in paper or digital form. (Matthew Bender & Co. v. West Publishing Co.,[73] 158 F.3d 674 (2d Cir. 1998), cert. denied, 119 S. Ct. 2039 (1999)).

3.2.4 Can a U.S. Government work be reused after it has been published in a non-government product?

Yes, U.S. Government works as originally submitted to the publisher (e.g., manuscripts, charts, photographs, etc.) may be reused in another publication.

3.2.5 Many U.S. Government employees are under the impression that they must transfer copyright in works prepared as part of their job to the publisher of a journal or book in order to have an article published. Is this true?

No, a paper, report, or other work prepared by an employee of the U.S. Government as part of that person's official duties is a U.S. Government work. Copyright protection is not provided for U.S. Government works under U.S. Copyright Law. Therefore, there is no U.S. Copyright to be transferred. U.S Government employees should inform the publisher of their employment status and should not sign any document purporting to transfer a U.S. copyright as a prerequisite to publication.

Additionally, a U.S. Government work may be protected under foreign copyright laws. The law of the foreign country governs ownership of foreign copyrights in U.S. Government works. The owner of the copyright may license or transfer a foreign copyright. The transfer of a foreign copyright owned by the U.S. Government must be executed by an authorized official of the Agency, who is almost never the U.S. Government author.

3.2.6 Should U.S. Government employees sign publishing agreements on works produced as part of their official duties?

Many publishers have standard forms that provide a specific space for authors to indicate that they are U.S. Government employees or that they are working on the Government's behalf. For examples, see the IEEE Copyright Form[74] and the Kluwer Academic/Plenum Publishing Transfer of Copyright Form[75].

However, many publishing agreements include other terms, such as indemnification or choice of law that the government employee may not have authority to accept. Employees should seek approval from their own organizations before signing such agreements.

The following is an example of wording for a permission form from the National Library of Medicine that can be suggested to a publisher.

The U.S. Copyright Act provides that federal government employees cannot copyright material prepared in the course of their employment. As an employee of the [name department or agency], I have no copyright interest to assign, and upon the recommendation of the Office of General Counsel, [acronym for department or agency], must decline to sign the copyright assignment.

Although for the above reasons I am technically unable to assign any copyright to [name publication], I still request and authorize you to publish the submitted article in accordance with your standard editorial policies. I hope this letter will be sufficient authorization for your needs to enable you to consider it favorably.

3.2.7 Is a work co-authored by a U.S. Government employee and a non-government author copyrightable?

A "joint work" is a work prepared by two or more authors with the intention that their contributions be merged into inseparable or interdependent parts of a unitary whole (see 17 USC § 101.[76]). The authors of a joint work are co-owners of the copyright in the work, unless there is an agreement to the contrary (see 17 USC § 201.[77]).

If a joint work is interdependent, contributions are generally created independently by separate co-authors with the intention to merge them into a unitary whole, and therefore they comprise separable parts. One should be able to isolate the contributions of a government employee from the contributions of a non-government employee. If, on the other hand, co-authors collaborated on much or all of a joint work, it will be considered inseparable, and it may be impossible to determine where the contributions of one author end and the other author or authors begin. Therefore, for an inseparable joint work, it is difficult or impossible to isolate the contribution of government employees from contributions of non-government employees. When the U.S. Government is joint author with a non-government entity, the law on how much of the work is protected by copyright is unsettled and is thus open to differing interpretations. In such situations, you should consult your Office of General Counsel.

Moreover, while the Copyright law provides that authors of a joint work are co-owners of the work, the law regarding how much the Government, as a joint author, may own is unsettled and thus open to differing interpretations. The notes following section 201 of the Copyright Act (17 U.S.C §201) state that, "Under the bill, as under current law, co-owners of a copyright would be treated generally as tenants in common, with each co-owner having an independent right to use or license the use of a work, subject to a duty of accounting to the other for any profits." Nonetheless, to protect the Government's interests, it would be prudent to obtain a license from the non-government co-owner to use and distribute the work.

Since joint authorship is a collaboration in which the authors have the intent from the beginning to create an integrated work, when it is anticipated that a government employee will participate as a joint author of a work arising under a contract or assistant agreement, it is advisable to consult your General Counsel and the outside author concerning the unsettled nature of the law.

4.0 WORKS CREATED UNDER A FEDERAL GOVERNMENT CONTRACT OR GRANT

4.1 If a Work Was Created Under a Government Contract, Who Holds the Copyright?

Unlike works of the U.S. Government, works produced by contractors under government contracts are protected under U.S. Copyright Law. (See Schnapper v. Foley, 667 F.2d 102 (D.C. Cir. 1981), cert. denied, 455 U.S. 948 (1982).) The ownership of the copyright depends on the terms of the contract. Contract terms and conditions vary between civilian agencies or NASA and the military.

Civilian agencies and NASA are guided by the Federal Acquisition Regulations (FAR)[78]. There are a number of FAR provisions that can affect the ownership of the copyright (see also FAQ Section 4.2 on data rights in SBIR contracts and Section 4.6 on the data rights for special works). FAR Subpart 27.4--Rights in Data and Copyrights[79] provides copyright guidance for the civilian agencies and NASA. In addition, Agencies may have their own FAR Supplements that should be followed.

Under the FAR general data rights clause (FAR 52.227-14),[80] except for works in which the contractor asserts claim to copyright, the Government has unlimited rights in all data first produced in the performance of a contract and all data delivered under a contract unless provided otherwise in the contract. Unless provided otherwise by an Agency FAR Supplement, a contractor may, without prior approval of the Contracting Officer, assert claim to copyright in scientific and technical articles based on or containing data first produced in the performance of a contract and published in academic, technical or professional journals, symposia proceedings, or the like. The express written permission of the Contracting Officer is required before the contractor may assert or enforce the copyright in all other works first produced in the performance of a contract. However, if a contract includes Alternate IV of the clause, the Contracting Officer's approval is not required to assert claim to copyright. Whenever the contractor asserts claim to copyright in works other than computer software, the Government, and others acting on its behalf, are granted a license to reproduce, prepare derivative works, distribute, perform and display the copyrighted work. For computer software the scope of the Government's license does not include the right to distribute to the public (see FAQ Section 4.3).

Occasionally there may be a special provision outside the FAR clauses that addresses data rights (this would also cover databases), but such provisions would have to be included in the contract, statement of work or other agreement that is in place. The specific language should be discussed with the Contracting Officer.

The Department of Defense (DoD) is guided by the Defense Federal Acquisition Regulation Supplement (DFARS) Subpart 227.71 [81]and Part 211[82] and Part 252[83] provisions that affect the ownership of copyright for works created under contract. DFARS Subpart 227.72 [84] provides the copyright guidance for DoD (FAR 27.400[85]). The DFARS recognizes that the contractor owns the copyright for works created under contract (DFARS 227.7103-9[86], DFARS 252.227-7013-4)[87]. If a special clause is inserted into a contract (DFARS 252.227-7020[88]), the contractor must assign the copyright to the Government.

While the Government has rights in more than just deliverables, as a practical matter the Government may have difficulty getting access to data unless it is either a deliverable or the contractor publishes it with a notice acknowledging the Government's sponsorship. The FAR requires an acknowledgment of Government sponsorship for contractor publications (see FAQ Sections 4.3 and 4.8). However, the DFARS does not. Therefore, it is advisable that works in which the Government desires rights are identified in the contract as deliverables. For software applications, the contract terms and conditions should also specify the format for delivery. If the Government needs to maintain or further develop the software program, it should consider expressly requiring delivery of source code.

4.2 Are Data Rights Any Different Under Special Programs Such as the Small Business Innovative Research (SBIR) Program?

Yes. In some cases, the particular program, such as the SBIR program, includes special copyright provisions. The FAR SBIR data rights clause, 52.227-20[89] permits an SBIR contractor to assert copyright ownership unless there is specific language in the contract to the contrary. If claim to copyright is made, the Government gets the same license as it receives under the FAR general data rights clause, 52.227-11 (see FAQ Section 4.3). Additional restrictions on the Governments use of SBIR Data may apply. SBIR data is data first produced by an SBIR contractor in the performance of an SBIR contract that is not generally known and that is not already available to the Government or has not been made available to others without an obligation of confidentiality. If SBIR Data delivered to the Government is marked with the SBIR Rights Notice provided in the clause, the Government may use the data for government purposes only, and cannot disclose the data outside the Government (except for use by support contractors) for a specified period of time. This additional restriction is intended to provide incentives for the development or commercialization of the technology or product by the private partner.

4.3 If the Contractor is allowed to Assert Copyright in a Work Produced Under a Government Contract, What Rights Does the Government Have?

A contractor's assertion of copyright in a work produced under a DFARS contract does not provide any restrictions to the Government's use of the work (see DFARS 227.7103-9[90] and 227.7203-9[91]). In a FAR contract, if the contractor is permitted to assert copyright, the Government will acquire a license to the copyrighted work. The extent of the license may depend on the type of work created (see FAR 52.227-14[92]).

Under the FAR, when a contractor asserts copyright in a work first produced in the performance of a contract with a civilian agency or NASA, the contractor must place a copyright notice acknowledging the government sponsorship (including contract number) on the work when it is delivered to the Government, as well as when it is published or deposited for registration with the U.S. Copyright Office (see FAQ Section 4.8). If no copyright notice is placed on the work, the Government obtains unlimited rights in the work. Unlimited rights allow the Government to provide the work to another contractor and distribute the work to the public, including posting the work to a public web site. Otherwise, when claim to copyright is made the Contractor grants the Government, and others acting on its behalf, a license to the work.

The Government's license is a nonexclusive, irrevocable, worldwide license to use, modify, reproduce, release, perform, display or disclose the work by or on behalf of the Government. The Government may use the work within the Government without restriction, and may release or disclose the work outside the Government and authorize persons to whom release or disclosure has been made to use, modify, reproduce, release, perform, display, or disclose the work on behalf of the government. The Government's license includes the right to distribute copies of the work to the public for government purpose. While the contractor may assign its copyright in "scientific and technical articles based on or containing data first produced in the performance of a contract" to a publisher, the Government's license rights attach to the articles upon creation and later assignment by the contractor to a publisher are subject to these rights. Under some FAR data rights clauses, if the work is a computer program, the right to release or disclose the computer program to the public is not included in the Government's license. If there is any question as to the scope of the Government's license, the Contracting Officer or your General Counsel should be consulted.

An example of a copyright statement, which includes a government license, for use with works created under contracts with civilian agencies and NASA is:

COPYRIGHT STATUS: This work, authored by _______________ employees, was funded in whole or in part by ___________________ under U.S. Government contract _______________, and is, therefore, subject to the following license: The Government is granted for itself and others acting on its behalf a paid-up, nonexclusive, irrevocable worldwide license in this work to reproduce, prepare derivative works, distribute copies to the public, and perform publicly and display publicly, by or on behalf of the Government. All other rights are reserved by the copyright owner.

4.4 Does the Government Have the Same Rights to Use Copyrighted Material Produced Outside of a Government Contract But Included in a Work Produced Under a Government Contract as it Does to Portions of the Work First Produced in Performance of the Contract?

It depends. Under both the FAR and the DFARS, the contractor may not include copyrighted material in the work created for the Government without identifying the copyrighted material to the Contracting Officer and obtaining the Contracting Officer's permission to incorporate the copyrighted material. Normally, the contractor provides a license to the copyrighted material equivalent to the license set forth in the contract. However, the contracting officer may approve a license of more limited scope if appropriate (see FAR 27.404(f)(2)[93] and DFARS 227.7103-9(a)(2)[94]).

4.5 May a Government Contractor Voluntarily Transfer Its Copyright to the Government?

Yes. The Government is not precluded from receiving and holding copyrights transferred to it by assignment. (See 17 USC § 105) A Copyright assigned or otherwise transferred to the Government does not lose its copyright status or protection. The Government may record transfers of copyright with the U.S. Copyright Office and may register copyrights transferred to it.

4.6 Can a Contractor Be Forced to Transfer Its Copyright to the Government?

Yes. Under the FAR special works data rights clause, 52.227-17,[95] in addition to requiring the Contracting Officer's written permission before a contractor may assert copyright ownership in material first produced under the contract, the Contracting Officer may instead direct the contractor to assign the copyright to the Government. Additionally, in accordance with FAR Section 27.404(g)(3)[96], agencies may, to the extent provided in their FAR supplements, place limitations or restrictions on the contractor's right to use, release to others, reproduce, distribute, or publish any data first produced in the performance of the contract, including a requirement to assign copyright to the Government. Thus, Agency FAR supplements (e.g., the NASA FAR Supplement at 1852.227-14[97] may also direct contractors in this way.

DFARS clause 252.227-7020[98] automatically directs the contractor to assign the copyright to the Government.

4.7 May a Contractor Use Works It Produced Under a Government Contract?

Yes, in most cases a contractor may use works it produced under a government contract. However, depending on the data rights clause in the contract, restrictions may apply. Under the FAR general data rights clause, 52.227-14,[99] the contractor must obtain authorization from the Contracting Officer to assert claim to copyright in a work created under the contract or no copyright may be asserted (see FAQ Section 4.1). However, in either situation, the contractor shall have the right to use, release to others, reproduce, distribute, or publish any data first produced or specifically used by the contractor in the performance of the contract, except to the extent such data may be subject to the federal export control or national security laws or regulations, may include restrictive markings or notices, or unless otherwise set forth in the contract (see FAR 27.404(g)[100] and 52.227-14(d)[101]). Agency FAR supplements may include more restrictive terms including the right to require the contractor to assign the copyright to the Government.

Under the FAR special works data rights clause 52.227-17[102], the contractor shall not use any work first produced in the performance of the contract for purposes other than the performance of the contract, nor shall the contractor release, reproduce, distribute, or publish any such work, nor authorize others to do so, without written permission of the Contracting Officer.

Likewise, DFARS clause 252.227-7013[103] recognizes the contractor's copyright, while DFARS clause 252.227-7020 [104] directs the contractor to assign the copyright to the Government. However, DFARS 227.7106(b)[105] notes that a contractor "retains use and disclosure rights" even after such an assignment. Therefore, the Government must negotiate a special license if it wishes to restrict a contractor's use of works it produced under contract. There may be other restrictions to the contractor's use, such as export control, national security, etc.

4.8 Must a Contractor Place a Copyright Notice or Acknowledgement of the Government's Rights and Sponsorship on a Work Produced Under Government Contract?

Yes, the FAR requires that any contractor claiming copyright ownership to material first produced under a FAR contract affix the copyright notice and acknowledgement of government sponsorship (including the contract number) on all copies delivered to the Government, on all published copies, and on all copies deposited with the U.S. Copyright Office (See FAR 27.404(f)(1)(v)[106]), although the Copyright Law has no copyright notice requirement for works created on or after March 1, 1989. If these notices are not affixed, the Government has unlimited rights. See FAQ Section 4.3 for an example of a copyright statement for use with works created under civilian agency and NASA contracts.

Under the DFARS, a copyright notice is not required. (See DFARS 252.227-7013(f) and 252.227-7014(f)[107].

4.9 What Are the Rules Regarding Works Produced Under Government Grants and Cooperative Agreements?

The data rights clauses in grants and cooperative agreements are flexible but generally allow the recipient to assert copyright. For works created under grants and cooperative agreements with colleges, universities, hospitals and non-profit organizations, all federal agencies adhere to the policies of OMB Circular A-110 Uniform Administrative Requirements for Grants and Agreements With Institutions of Higher Education, Hospitals, and Other Non-Profit Organizations[108] and to OMB Circular A-102, Grants and Cooperative Agreements with State and Local Governments[109] when the grantee is a state or local agency such as a state university. Section 36 of Circular A-110[110] provides that a grantee may assert copyright in any work that was developed under the grant or cooperative agreement. The Federal awarding agency reserves a royalty-free, nonexclusive and irrevocable right to reproduce, publish, or otherwise use the work for federal purposes, and to authorize others to do so. It should be noted that new requirements for providing government access[111]to information created from grants and cooperative agreements were passed as part of the 1999 Omnibus Spending Bill.

Agencies may follow other policies with grants and cooperative agreements with commercial firms. The terms of the particular grant or cooperative agreement will specify respective rights of the parties. Which data rights clause is in the grant or cooperative agreement, and its specific language, should be discussed with the Grants Officer or your General Counsel.

4.10 If the grantee assigns his copyright in scientific and technical articles produced under a Government grant to a publisher, what rights does the Government have in the article?

Pursuant to Section 36 of OMB Circular A-110(a)[112], "the Federal awarding agency(ies) reserve a royalty-free, nonexclusive and irrevocable right to reproduce, publish, or otherwise use the work for Federal purposes, and to authorize others to do so." The Government's license rights attach to the articles and later assignment by the grantee to a publisher are subject to these rights.

4.11 If the contractor assigns his copyright in scientific and technical articles produced under a Government contract to a publisher, what rights does the Government had in the article?

The Government's license rights attach to "scientific and technical articles based on or containing data first produced in the performance of a contract and published in academic, technical or professional journals, symposia proceedings or similar works" (See FAR Clause 52.227.14 Rights in Data General[113] as prescribed in 27.409(a)[114]). Later assignment by the contractor to a publisher are subject to these rights.

The Contractor grants to the Government, and others acting on its behalf, a paid-up, nonexclusive, irrevocable worldwide license to reproduce, prepare derivative works, distribute copies to the public, and perform publicly and display publicly, by or on behalf of the Government.

4.12 What Language could be used in a copyright agreement between a contractor or grantee author and a publisher to clarify the author's right to deposit journal

articles in the electronic repository of the government agency that funded the author's research?

In 2005 the National Institutes of Health (NIH) implemented a Policy on Enhancing Public Access to Archived Publications Resulting from NIH-Funded Research[115]. The NIH Policy explicitly recognizes and upholds the principles of copyright. Authors and journals can continue to assert copyright in NIH-funded scientific publications, in accordance with current practice. The policy encourages authors to exercise their right to give NIH a copy of their final manuscript before publication. While individual copyright arrangements can take many forms, NIH encourages investigators to sign agreements that specifically allow the manuscript to be deposited with NIH for public posting on PubMed Central[116] as soon as possible after journal publication. Institutions and investigators may wish to develop particular contract terms in consultation with their own legal counsel, as appropriate. But, as an example, the kind of language that an author or institution might add to a copyright agreement includes the following: "Journal acknowledges that Author retains the right to provide a copy of the final manuscript to NIH upon acceptance for Journal publication or thereafter, for public archiving in PubMed Central as soon as possible after publication by Journal."

5.0 USE OF COPYRIGHTED WORKS

5.1 Use of Non-Government Copyrighted Works in a U.S. Government Work

5.1.1 Does the U.S. Government have any special rights to use copyrighted material?

No, the U.S. Government can be held liable for violation of the Copyright Laws. Congress has expressly provided that a work protected by the Copyright Laws can be infringed by the United States (28 USC § 1498(b))[117]. The exclusive action for such infringement is an action by the copyright owner against the United States in the Court of Federal Claims for the recovery of monetary damages. However, there is no contributory copyright infringement on the part of the Government because it hasn't waived sovereign immunity rights. (John C. Boyle, 200 F.3d 1369 (Fed. Cir. 2000)[118].

While the Government may rely on fair use, the use of materials by the Government is not automatically a fair use. The U.S. Department of Justice, Office of Legal Counsel, has stated in a U.S. Department of Justice opinion dated April 30, 1999,[119] that "while government reproduction of copyrighted material for governmental use would in many contexts be non-infringing because it would be a 'fair use' under 17 USC § 107, there is no 'per se' rule under which such government reproduction of copyrighted material invariably qualifies as a fair use."

Single copy reproduction of portions of a copyrighted work for use solely for official research or related purposes is ordinarily permissible. Additionally, there may be limited exceptions in the case of National Security where the public interest results in a privilege to the Government for use of the copyrighted work without the express consent of the copyright owner. (Key Maps, Inc. v. Pruitt, 470 F. Supp. 33 (S.D. Tex. 1978)) For further discussion, see "Application of the Copyright Doctrine of Fair Use to the Reproduction of Copyrighted Material for Intelligence Purposes"[120] by Major Gary M. Bowen. The Army Lawyer (DA Pam 27-50-332), July 2000.

5.1.2 Are there any copyright issues related to the use of non-government citations or abstracts in U.S. Government authored bibliographies or databases?

Individual citations are considered facts and are not protected by copyright. However, a collection of citations may have protection as a compilation. (See FAQ Section 2.1.4)

Government use of abstracts from copyrighted sources in abstracting and indexing (A&I) services or bibliographic databases should first look to any existing license agreements between the agency and the A&I service. The A&I service may have a license agreement with the publisher for use of copyrighted information for specific purposes. However, in most cases, the A&I service does not have the right to transfer this permission to subsequent users. Therefore, if abstracts are to be used in a published bibliography, it is best to seek the permission of the copyright owners.

5.1.3 Does copyrighted material lose its copyright status and protection if it becomes part of a U.S. Government work or is included in a compilation published by the Government?

No, copyrighted material contained in a U.S. Government work does not lose its copyright status and protection. The copyright status of non-government works in a compilation is not affected by the lack of copyright protection of other works in the compilation or by the fact that the U.S. Government publishes the compilation. When copyrighted materials are included in a Government work or a compilation published by the Government, a copyright notice indicating what portions of the work are protected by copyright, and identifying the copyright owner, should be included. (See Copyright Office Circular 1[121])

5.1.4 May the U.S. Government use works of foreign governments or international organizations?

Many foreign countries provide copyright protection for works of their government. However, certain types of official works of government bodies, such as statutes and court decisions, are generally not copyrighted. Many foreign governments will consider waiving copyright upon request.

International organizations, such as the United Nations and the World Bank, also hold copyright. However, many of these documents may contain waivers or waivers may be obtained upon request. Depending on the particular agreement, the U.S. Government may have additional rights based on contributing, paying or being a sponsoring member of the organization.

5.1.5 Can the Government translate a copyrighted work to which it does not hold copyright?

Translations are considered derivative works and whether the translation of the work is fair use should be evaluated based on the fair use factors provided in the Copyright Law at 17 U.S.C. § 107[122] (See FAQ Section 2.2.2).

5.2 Use of Government Libraries and Archives

5.2.1 Are there any special policies that apply to Government libraries and archives?

No, there are no special policies that apply to Government libraries and archives. However, under 17 USC § 108[123], all libraries and archives are provided special rights with respect to interlibrary loan, archiving and preservation.

"It is not an infringement of copyright for a library or archives, or any of its employees acting within the scope of their employment, to reproduce no more than one copy or phonorecord of a work, or to distribute such copy or phonorecord, under the conditions specified by this section, if the…

1. reproduction or distribution is made without any purpose of direct or indirect commercial advantage;
2. collections of the library or archives are (i) open to the public, or (ii) available not only to researchers affiliated with the library or archives or with the institution of which it is a part, but also to other persons doing research in a specialized field; and

3. reproduction or distribution of the work includes a notice of copyright."

Specific guidelines on photocopying and interlibrary loan are also provided in the CONTU Guidelines on Photocopying under Interlibrary Loan Arrangements,[124] and in Copyright Office Circular 21: Reproductions of Copyrighted Works by Educators and Librarians.[125]

5.2.2 Can copyrighted materials be copied for library archival purposes?

Section 108 of the Copyright Act[126] addresses library archiving. The Digital Millennium Copyright Act[3] amended Sec. 108 to cover both digital and non-digital copies. It permits the creation of three copies only if the library or archives has, after reasonable effort, determined that an unused replacement cannot be obtained at a reasonable price. These copies may not be distributed to the public outside the premises of the library or archive. The material may also be converted to a new format for preservation.

Although, the Sonny Bono Copyright Term Extension Act added 20 years to the term of copyright, it also added section 108(h), allowing libraries and archives to make copies of text works that were no longer being sold and copies of which cannot be obtained at a reasonable price for preservation purposes during the 20-year extension period. Title IV "Preservation of Orphan Works Act" contained in the " The Family Entertainment and Copyright Act of 2005" amends section 108(i) and 108(h) to now include musical works; pictorial, graphical and sculptural works; and most motion pictures and other audiovisual works.

5.2.3 What happens if the actual need for copyrighted material exceeds the exceptions granted in 17 USC §§ 107 and 108?

When the anticipated needs for copyrighted material exceed the exceptions granted in § 107[127] and §108[128], then the agency, library or the patron should seek permission or license agreements. Two approaches to managing these permissions and licenses are to enter into an agreement with the copyright owner directly or to establish an agreement with a copyright clearance center (see FAQ Section 6).

5.2.4 Do copyright principles apply to materials purchased and licensed by Government libraries?

Federal librarians procure published materials in a variety of formats for the use of federal employees and the public. Generally, federal libraries do not own copyrights in the materials in their collection. In the paper environment, libraries usually purchase copies to add to their collections. Copyright law, fair use, and the "first sale" doctrine address the rights and responsibilities of the library as purchaser and of its users. However, in the digital environment, while copyright principles apply, the rights of the library and its users are usually negotiated through contractual agreements and licenses. The terms of these agreements usually allow viewing materials and making reasonable copies for personal or agency use.

Most specifically forbid:

1. Substantial or systematic reproduction.
2. Systematic supply or distribution to non-authorized users.

It is important to work with your agency contracting officer and legal advisor in negotiating license agreements for databases, e-books, electronic journals or other subscription products. For further discussion and guidance, see the FEDLINK video presentation Licensing Electronic Publications for Use in a Federal Agency[129], CENDI's License Agreements for Electronic Products and Services: Frequently Asked Questions[130], and the National Library of Medicine Policy on Acquiring Copyrighted Material in Electronic Format[131].

Libraries should be proactive in informing and educating users about copyright and information license agreements. For examples, see the Naval Research Laboratory Library Use and Disclaimer Notice[132] and Smithsonian Institution Libraries Permissions: Using Digital Materials from the Smithsonian Institution Libraries[133].

5.3 Permissions, Licenses, and releases to Use Copyrighted Works

5.3.1 How can you determine if copyright permission is needed?

Permission is not needed if the work is in the public domain (see FAQ Section 2.2.4), when the use is a fair use (see FAQ Section 2.2.2), or if a license or agreement covers the intended use. Otherwise, permission should be sought.

5.3.2 Is it necessary to get permission to use facts from a copyrighted source?

Permission is not needed for the use of facts, because Copyright Law does not protect facts. However, to the extent that the facts are presented in tables, chart, graphs, or figures that can be copyrighted, permission may be necessary. Although it is always desirable to give attribution to the source, attribution is not a substitute for permission.

5.3.3 What should be considered when getting a license, release or permission?

Reasonable rights should be requested, covering the uses for which the work is intended to be utilized and considering potential uses in the future. Copyright owners generally treat permissions as being more informal than licenses. Permissions are usually royalty-free, so the rights requested should be reasonably narrow. However, licenses and releases often require a royalty or one-time payment. In all cases, consideration should be given to platforms/formats, geographical or marketing areas, duration, warranties and indemnities for incorrect information, one-time only or multiple uses, and current version versus revisions.

The wording should be developed with your Office of General Counsel. However, the final product will be only as comprehensive as the information you have provided to the counsel concerning your intended use of the material.

Many publishers have examples of permissions posted. A sample letter requesting permission is available from the University of Texas.[134]

5.3.4 Are there other rights that should be addressed regarding the U.S. Government's use of non-government works?

Yes, these may include the rights of privacy and publicity. For example, a release should be sought in all cases where a person's voice or recognizable image will be included in the Government work. While a release may have been obtained for one purpose, it may not necessarily cover additional uses. If authorization to use a picture or video for government purposes is obtained, use for non-governmental purposes may require additional authorization. For example, if a picture or video is being provided to a commercial firm for commercial use, the original release may not apply. Your General Counsel should review the original release.

5.3.5 Can the Government transfer licenses or permissions?

The ability to transfer permission depends on the original agreement between the copyright owner and the party to which the permission was originally granted. Permission obtained from a copyright owner is not transferable to a third party, unless expressly stated. If a Government agency has obtained a government-wide permission, it may provide the material to other agencies.

5.3.6 Must the Government request permission to include copyrighted material owned by a government employee in a U.S. Government work?

Yes. The Government or any other entity wishing to include copyrighted materials in a publication must seek permission from any copyright owner (See FAQ Section 5.1.1). For limitations on a government employees' right to sue the Government for copyright infringement, see 28 U.S.C. § 1498(b)[135].

5.3.7 Does a government agency need a license to perform copyrighted music or show a copyrighted video at a government sponsored meeting or event?

The agency may not need a license if the event is not open to the public and less than a substantial number of persons may attend; if the performance falls within fair use; or if the performance of the copyrighted work is in the course of face-to-face teaching or is otherwise exempt under § 110[136].

This question primarily involves whether or not this is a "public performance." 17 U.S.C. § 106(4)[137] provides the copyright owner with the exclusive right to "perform the copyrighted work publicly," but this exclusive right does not extend to private performances, and the agency may show the video if the performance were considered to be private. "Public performance" means: 1) to perform or display a work at a public place or any place where a substantial number of persons (other than a family and its social circle) are gathered; or 2) to transmit or communicate a performance or display to a place specified in (1) or to the public, regardless of whether the performance or display is received in one or more places and at the same time or at different times, see 17 U.S.C. § 101[138].

With respect to a "substantial number of persons," The House Committee on the Judiciary Report to accompany S.22, which became the Copyright Act of October 1976, P.L. 94-553, 90 Stat. 2541, indicated that routine meetings of businesses and governmental personnel would be excluded because they do not represent the gathering of a "substantial number of persons." See H.R. Rep. No. 1476, 94th Cong.2d Sess. 64, reprinted in 1976 U.S. Code Cong. & Adm. News 5659, 5677-78[139].

The House Report, however, is not the law, although a court might look to it if it found the law to be ambiguous and that the Report helped explain Congress's intent concerning the ambiguity; further, the Report is arguably inconsistent with the statutory language's reference to a family and its social circle. See Patry on Copyright, §14:25[140]. Rather than relying on this statement in the House Report, all aspects of the intended use, intended audience, and location of the performance should be examined.

Neither the law nor the House Report defines a "substantial number of persons," and the House Report does not define "routine meeting." However, the fewer the number of attendees and more often the gatherings take place, the more likely a meeting is to be "routine" and to have fewer than "a substantial number" of persons. Note that the meeting is what must be routine; routine copyright violations are not permitted.

Regardless of the audience's size, events that are open to the public usually constitute a "public performance," even if the performance occurs in a private or "semipublic place," such as an office. See Columbia Pictures Industries[141], Inc. v. Redd Horne Inc, 568 F.Supp 494 (W.D.Pa. 1983) aff'd 749 F.2d 154 (3d Cir, 1984). In this case the court found it unnecessary to consider whether a substantial number of people were gathered, finding that the video booths in question were "open to the public" and citing H.R.Rep. No. 1476, 94th Cong.2d Sess. 64, "One of the principal purposes of the definition [of "publicly"] was to make clear that, contrary to the decision in Metro-Goldwyn-Mayer Distributing Corp. v. Wyatt, 21 C.O. Bull. 203 (D. Md. 1932), performances in 'semipublic' places such as clubs, lodges, factories, summer camps, and schools are 'public performances' subject to copyright control."

Notwithstanding 17 U.S.C. § 106[142], a public performance may be a "fair use" of a copyrighted work, see 17 U.S.C. § 107[143]. Whether or not a group charges an admission fee for the event is not determinative as to whether there is a copyright violation: in addition to the effect on the market for the work, the purpose of the use, nature of the work, and amount of the work (such as a video clip vs. the whole video) that is performed are also key considerations. For guidance on "fair use," see FAQ Section 2.2.2.

Performance of a work by instructors or pupils in the course of face-to-face teaching activities of a nonprofit educational institution, in a classroom or similar place devoted to instruction does not infringe copyright, see 17 U.S.C. § 110(1)[144]. Non-dramatic literary or music works, such as certain nonprofit musical performances, may also be performed without permission under specific circumstances. See, e.g., § 110(4)[145].

5.4 Infringement by the Government

5.4.1 What acts constitute a copyright infringement?

Unauthorized use of a copyrighted work is an infringement unless the use is outside the exclusive rights provided by the Copyright Law, or unless the use is covered by one of the limitations on the exclusive right, such as fair use under 17 U.S.C. § 107[146], reproduction by libraries or archives under 17 U.S.C. § 108[147], or transfer of particular copies or phonorecords (first sale doctrine) under 17 U.S.C. §109[148]. Once the copyright is registered in the U.S. Copyright Office, the owner of the exclusive rights infringed is entitled to institute an infringement action.

5.4.2 Can a copyright owner sue the Government if the Government or a contractor performing under a government contract, infringes the copyright?

Yes. Title 28 U.S.C. § 1498(b)[149] specifies that a copyright owner's exclusive remedy shall be an action against the United States in the U.S. Court of Federal Claims. The suit must be initiated within three years of the act of infringement. The U.S. Government is also liable for infringement by a government contractor if the contractor acted with the authorization or consent of the Government. DOD agencies process administrative claims of copyright infringement in accordance with DFARS Subpart 227.70[150].

5.4.3 What are the consequences for infringement by U.S. Government agencies?

In accordance with 28 U.S.C. 1498(b)[151], the Government's liability is for either the reasonable and entire compensation or the minimum statutory damages. The minimum statutory damages are $750 per infringement. Therefore, neither willful nor innocent infringement is an issue when determining damages for the Government.

5.4.4 Who represents the government in copyright infringement suits?

The Department of Justice represents the government in court.

6.0 APPLICABLE COPYRIGHT LEGISLATION AND OTHER RESOURCES ON THE INTERNET

(originally published as Bibliography on Copyright: Education and Fair Use Issues, 12/26/00, used courtesy of Mary Levering, U.S. Copyright Office)

This bibliography lists some recent publications, articles, brochures, websites, and listservs related to copyright educational and library fair use issues that provide information and a variety of perspectives on these issues. This list is not intended to be exhaustive nor does the U.S. Copyright Office necessarily endorse the work listed. Website addresses cited were all correct and active as of August 2004.

U.S. Copyright Office Sources

U.S. Copyright Office. Copyright Act of 1976, as amended.
[http://www.copyright.gov/title17/] [U.S. Copyright Law. 17 U.S.C. §§ 101, et seq.]

U.S. Copyright Office. *Copyright Basics*. Circular 1, 1996. 12 pp.
[http://www.copyright.gov/circs/circ1.html] [Copyright Office Circular 1 provides general information and answers some basic questions that are frequently asked about copyright.]

U.S. Copyright Office. *Fair Use*, FL 102 (form letter), June 1999. 1 p.
[http://www.copyright.gov/fls/fl102.html] [Form letter summarizing basic fair use principles.]

U.S. Copyright Office. *DMCA Section 104 Report*, August 2001. 166 pp. plus appendices
[http://www.copyright.gov/reports/studies/dmca/dmca_study.html]
[This Report, pursuant to § 104 of the Digital Millennium Copyright Act,
describes the effects of DMCA's Title 1 and the development of electronic commerce and associated technology on the operation of 2 sections of the Copyright Act which limit exclusive rights (§ 109 "effect of transfer of particular copy or phonorecord" and § 117 "computer programs" of Title 17 U.S.C, as amended); the report evaluates the relationships between existing and emerging technology and the operation of these sections.]

U.S. Copyright Office. *Report on Copyright and Digital Distance Education*, May 1999. 170 pp. Plus appendices.

[http://www.copyright.gov/disted/]
[This report gives an overview of the nature of distance education as of mid-'99, describes licensing practices in digital distance education (including problems and future trends), the status of technologies relating to delivery of distance education courses and protection of their content; discusses prior initiatives to address copyright issues through negotiation of guidelines or enactment of legislation, and analyzes the application of Copyright Law to digital distance education.]
U.S. Copyright Office. *Reproduction of Copyrighted Works by Educators and Librarians*. Circular 21, 1992. 26 pp.
http://www.copyright.gov/circs/circ21.pdf]
[This circular includes excerpts from pertinent Congressional documents and legislative provisions relating to fair use and library photocopying in the U.S. Copyright Law, and other relevant documents dealing with reproduction of copyrighted works by librarians and educators. It includes the 4 sets of educational and library fair use guidelines incorporated in U.S. congressional documents in 1976 and 1981.]
U.S. Copyright Office. *Website*.
[http://www.copyright.gov/]
[Most of the information published by the U.S. Copyright Office on paper is also available for viewing and downloading from the Office's website and gopher site, including information circulars, federal copyright regulations, the Register's testimony, the Office's recent major reports, application forms, and access to Copyright Office records from 1978. To access Copyright Office online databases of copyright records, use (telnet: locis.loc.gov).]

CONFU (Conference on Fair Use, 1994-98)

U.S. Information Infrastructure Task Force, Working Group on Intellectual Property Rights, Bruce Lehman, Chair. T*he Conference on Fair Use: Report to the Commissioner on the Conclusion of the Conference on*

Fair Use. Washington, DC. U.S. Patent and Trademark Office. 1998. 189 pp.
[http://www.uspto.gov/web/offices/dcom/olia/confu/confurep.pdf]
[The CONFU November 1998 Final Report and the September 1997 First Phase Report document the genesis and history of CONFU, contain proposals for educational fair use guidelines for distance learning (Appendix I), and for digital images (Appendix H), the guidelines adopted for educational multimedia, the uniform preamble accepted by CONFU participants (Appendix G), the "Statement on Use of Copyrighted Computer Programs (Software) in Libraries--Scenarios" (Appendix K), together with all of the individual comments and institutional notifications received concerning the proposals for guidelines and information about the participating organizations.]

Other Sources:

Association of Research Libraries. *Principles For Licensing Electronic Resources*. July 15, 1997. 6 pp.
[http://www.arl.org/sc/licensing/licprinciples.shtml]
[Six library associations, representing an international membership of libraries of all types and sizes, developed this statement of principles to guide libraries in negotiating license agreements for access to electronic resources so as to create agreements that respect the rights and obligations of both parties.]
Besenjak, Cheryl. *Copyright Plain and Simple*. Franklin Lakes, NJ. Career Press, 1997. 192 pp.
[This handbook on copyright principles and procedures outlines the fundamental elements of copyright in plain and simple language and through practical examples as part of the Career Press "Plain and Simple" series.]
Bruwelheide, Janis H. and Mary Hutchings Reed. *The Copyright Primer for Librarians and Educators*. Chicago, IL: American Library Association, and Washington, DC: National Education Association, 2d edition, 1995. 160 pp.

[This resource for educators and librarians in a question-and-answer format offers commentary on critical developments, especially those related to video, digitization and emerging technology, addressing issues such as fair use, copyright and photocopying for library & educational purposes from an educator's perspective.]

Computer Science and Telecommunications Board, National Research Council. T*he Digital Dilemma: Intellectual Property in The Information Age*. Washington, DC. National Academy Press, 2000. 340 pp.
http://www.nap.edu/books/0309064996/html
[This report by the Committee on Intellectual Property Rights in the Emerging Information Infrastructure describes the multiple facets of digitized intellectual property, defining terms, identifying key issues, and explaining alternatives, and follows the complex threads of law, business, incentives to creators, the American tradition of access to information, the international context and the nature of human behavior. NAP announcement fall 2000.]

Consortium for Educational Technology for University Systems. *Fair Use of Copyrighted Works: A Crucial Element in Educating America*. Seal Beach, CA: CSU Chancellor's Office, 1995. 34 pp. [California State University, State University of New York, City University of New York.]
[http://www.cetus.org/fairindex.html]
[A consortium of three major universities, the CSU-SUNY-CUNY Work Group on Ownership, Legal Rights of Use, and Fair Use, address copyright and fair use in the context of higher education, includes analyses of court decisions on educational fair use.]

Crews, Kenneth D. *Copyright Essentials for Librarians and Educators*. Chicago, IL: American Library Association, 2000. 143 pp.
[This analysis by Kenneth Crews, with contributions from Dwayne K. Butler and others, was a project of the

Copyright Management Center of Indiana University - Purdue University (which is directed by Crews who serves as Associate Dean of the Faculties for Copyright Management) and is intended to help professionals that provide information to the public understand and apply copyright law, and make informed and appropriate decisions about protecting copyright when using new formats and delivery systems that make duplication and transfer of information so easy.]

Crews, Kenneth D. *Copyright Law and Graduate Research: New Media, New Rights and Your Dissertation*. Ann Arbor, MI: UMI Company, 1996. 29 pp.

[This useful manual explains the fundamentals of copyright and is intended to help university students and faculty advisors understand their legal rights and responsibilities regarding the use of others copyrighted works. It explains when to seek copyright permissions and how to obtain them and also provides guidance on how to protect one's own copyrighted works.]

Crews, Kenneth D. *Copyright, Fair Use, and the Challenge for Universities: Promoting the Progress of Higher Education*. Chicago, IL: The University of Chicago Press, 1993. 256 pp.

[An explanation of copyright and the ambiguous concepts of fair use as they affect and are affected by higher education. The first large-scale study of its kind surveys the copyright policies of 98 American research universities and reveals a variety of ways in which universities have responded to--and how they could better manage--the conflicting goals of copyright policies--avoiding infringements while promoting lawful uses that serve teaching and research. *Introduction*.]

Perspectives on ... Fair Use, Education, and Libraries: A Town Meeting to Examine the Conference on Fair Use. Lois Lunin, ed., Kenneth D. Crews and Dwayne K. Buttler, guest eds. Journal of the American Society for Information Science. Vol. 50, 1999.

[This special issue of JASIS Perspectives contains

several articles by presenters at the 2d town meeting on fair use, "Fair Use, Education and Libraries: a Town Meeting to Explore the Conference on Fair Use", hosted by the Indiana University Institute for the Study of Intellectual Property and Education and held at the campus of Indiana University-Purdue University in Indianapolis, Indiana, on April 4, 1997.]

Fair Use Guidelines for Educational Multimedia. Nonlegislative Report of the Subcommittee on Courts and Intellectual Property, Committee on the Judiciary, U.S. House of Representatives. September 27, 1996. 12 pp.
[http://www.ccumc.org/system/files/MMFUGuides.pdf]
[The Consortium of College and University Media Centers coordinated development of these guidelines during 1994-96, together with numerous participating organizations in a parallel initiative to CONFU; these guidelines were completed in September 1996 and acknowledged by the U.S. Congress in this Nonlegislative Report.]

Gasaway, Laura N., editor. *Growing Pains: Adapting Copyright for Libraries, Education and Society*. Littleton, CO: Fred B. Rothman & Co., 1997. 558 pp.
[Collection of 20 essays written by a variety of scholars with expertise in the fields of Copyright Law, education, and librarianship who advocate changes in the copyright statute, in interpretations of the law, and in school and library practices so that librarians and educators can meet their obligations.]

Gasaway, Laura N. and Sarah K. Wiant. *Libraries and Copyright: A Guide to Copyright Law in the 1990s*. Washington, DC: Special Libraries Association, 1994. 271 pp.
[Both authors are directors of university law libraries and professors of law; this source covers the functions and uses of Copyright Law, geared primarily to librarians and anyone engaged in the lending of and dissemination of copyrighted works.]

Goldstein, Paul. *Copyright's Highway: From Gutenburg to the Celestial Jukebox*. New York, NY: Hill and Wang, 1994. 261 pp.
[Copyright expert Paul Goldstein, Professor of Law at Stanford University, traces the 300-year old history of copyright, explains the concepts and rationale behind the idea of intellectual property rights, and highlights noteworthy legal battles, (including the famous Williams & Wilkins photocopying case). Booklist, Dec. 1, 1994.]
Hardy, I. Trotter. *Project Looking Forward: Sketching the Future of Copyright in a Networked World-Final Report*. Washington, DC: U.S. Copyright Office, May 1998. 304 pp.
[http://www.copyright.gov/reports/thardy.pdf]
[A report commissioned by the U.S. Copyright Office from I. Trotter Hardy, Professor of Law, College of William and Mary, as part of the U.S. Copyright Office's continuing effort to examine the future of the Internet and related digital communication's technologies, and to identify legal and policy issues that might arise as a result. Copies are available from the U.S. Government Printing Office - stock number 030-002-00191-8.]
Harper, Georgia. Will We Need Fair Use in the Twenty-First Century? March 4, 1997. 31 pp.
[http://www.utsystem.edu/ogc/intellectualproperty/fair_use.htm]
[The author, a copyright lawyer in the Office of General Counsel of the University of Texas System, explores the meaning of fair use to "focus attention on those parts of its function that are most affected by the electronic environment; an examination of that effect; an evaluation of the supposed benefits of fair use and alternative ways to achieve those benefits given the impact of the electronic environment on fair use."]
Malero, Marie C. *A Legal Primer on Managing Museum Collections*. Washington, DC: Smithsonian Institution Press, 2 ed. 1998.
[This source has an informative 50-page discussion on copyright issues for museums, written by former

Smithsonian Institution Assistant General Counsel Ildiko DeAngelis.]
Shapiro, Michael S. and Brent I. Miller. *A Museum Guide to Copyright and Trademark*. Washington, DC: American Association of Museums, 1999. 226 pp. [This Museum Guide is designed to guide informed decisions by museums about how to manage intellectual property owned by the museums and that of others that museums hold in trust, and how to establish best practices for developing institutional policy and procedural statements.]
Templeton, Brad. *10 Big Myths About Copyright Explained: An Attempt to Answer Common Myths About Copyright Seen on the Net*. [http://www.templetons.com/brad/copymyths.html] [This web-based essay by a publisher of an electronic newspaper on the net is an attempt to answer common "myths" about copyright seen on the Net and covers issues related to copyright and Usenet/Internet publication.]

Websites (with copyright information)

These websites contain references, inks, and additional informational resources and opinions on copyright, educational and library fair use issues. Many of these sites have links to other informational materials with related copyright themes.

Fair Use Guidelines for Educational Multimedia. [http://www.ccumc.org/copyright/ccguides.html] [Development of these fair use guidelines was coordinated by the Consortium of College and University Media Centers during 1994-96, together with numerous participating organizations. The guidelines were recognized by the U.S. Congress in a Nonlegislative Report dated September 27, 1996.]

Indiana University. Copyright Management Center. [http://www.copyright.iupui.edu/]

[Maintained as a resource for the academic community, this site offers access to resources about copyright and its importance to higher education. Topics of particular interest include fair use and distance learning.]

Library of Congress. American Memory: How to Understand Copyright Restrictions.
[http://memory.loc.gov/ammem/ndlpedu/start/cpyrt/index.html]
[The Library of Congress provides general information on copyright, fair use and questions related to classroom examples from teachers, using American Memory collections, digitized by the Library of Congress and available on the Library's website.]

Copyright for Music Librarians.
[http://www.lib.jmu.edu/org/mla/]
[MLA's website on copyright, "A Guide to Copyright for Music Librarians".]

Software and Information Industry Association.
[http://www.siia.net]
[SIIA, a trade association of the information industry, software developers and producers, conducts a comprehensive program of education, legal enforcement and public policy to fight the problem of software piracy; its education program provides tools for educators and others to help teach respect for copyright in software.]

Stanford University. [http://fairuse.stanford.edu/]
[http://palimpsest.stanford.edu/bytopic/intprop/]
[Websites on "Copyright and Fair Use" and "Copyright and Intellectual Property" with many documents and links related to libraries, education, copyright and fair use.]

University of Texas System. "Copyright Management Center Website."

[http://www.utsystem.edu/OGC/intellectualproperty/cprtindx.htm]
[Contains many resources related to copyright in libraries and includes an interactive "Software and Database License Agreement Checklist."]

Washington State University.
[http://publishing.wsu.edu/copyright/index.html]
[Website for the University's Copyright Office with links to articles, fact sheets, and guidelines on copyright.]

When Works Pass Into the Public Domain.
[http://www.unc.edu/~unclng/public-d.htm]
[This chart, compiled by Laura N. Gasaway, outlines the duration of copyright for works covered by U.S. Copyright Law.]

Yale University.
[http://www.library.yale.edu/~okerson/copyproj.html]
[Website with "Copyright Resources Online".]

Websites (for copyright licensing and permissions)
The following are some of the organizations that manage rights on behalf of rights holders and provide copyright licensing and permissions services. Others provide helpful information determining public domain works of for locating rights holders.

Art Museum Image Consortium (AMICO)
[http://www.amico.org/home.html]
[AMICO is a not-for-profit association of institutions with collections of art that have come together to enable educational use of the digital documentation in their collections through licensing educational access to museum multimedia documentation.]

Authors Registry.
[http://www.authorsregistry.org/]
[The Authors Registry is a non-exclusive licensor of

author or agent-controlled rights including electronic and photocopy reproduction rights.]

Christian Copyright Licensing International (CCLI).
[http://www.ccli.com]
[CCLI serves more than 140,000 churches worldwide to educate churches about Copyright Laws and provide licensing services for reproduction of church-related materials.]

Copyright Clearance Center (CCC).
[http://www.copyright.com/ccc/viewPage.do?pageCode=cr10-n]
[The CCC is a not-for-profit organization created in 1978 at the suggestion of the U.S. Congress to help organizations and individuals comply with U.S. Copyright Law through its licensing programs which provide authorized users with a lawful means for making photocopies from its repertory of over 1,750,000 titles.]

Creative Eye.
[http://creativeeyecoop.com]
[Creative Eye, a cooperative of independent photographers and illustrators,
provides licensing services for images in digital form on behalf of its members through its stock agency, Mira.]

Graphic Artists Guild (GAG).
[http://www.gag.org/]
[The GAG provides online portfolios of GAG members for permissions and licensing purposes]

Motion Picture Licensing Corporation (MPLC).
[http://www.mplc.com]
(MPLC is a copyright licensing service authorized by major Hollywood motion picture studios and independent producers to grant "umbrella" licenses to non-profit groups businesses and government

organizations for public performances of home videocassettes and videodiscs.]

Music performing rights licensing organizations.

ASCAP [http://www.ascap.com/licensing/about.html]

BMI [http://www.bmi.com/licensing/]

SESAC
[http://www.sesac.com/licensing/obtain_a_license.aspx]
[These music performing rights licensing organizations represent song writers and publishers and provide information about music licensing and copyrights.]

National Association of College Stores (NACS).
[http://www.nacs.org/public/industry.asp]
[The NACS website includes copyright information, Q&A concerning copyright compliance, procedures for obtaining permission to copy, including coursepack permission request forms and the guidelines for classroom copying.]

National Writers Union/Publications Rights Clearinghouse (NWU/PRC).
[http://www.nwu.org]
[The Publications Rights Clearinghouse is the NWU agency that collects online royalties for freelance writers.]

National Music Publishers Association/Harry Fox Agency (HFA).
[http://www.nmpa.org/aboutnmpa/hfa.asp]
[The HFA, which represents over 20,000 American music publishers, was established by the National Music Publishers Association to license musical compositions for use on records, tapes, audio-visual works, CDs and computer chips for private and commercial purposes.]

Picture Archive Council of America (PACA).
[http://www.pacaoffice.org/]
[PACA is the trade association for stock photography agencies in North America with almost 100 member agencies' names, addresses and contact information listed on the Website. Image users can request a complimentary copy of the PACA membership directory by fax to the PACA Office--fax# 507-645-7066 or by email [info@pacaoffice.org.]

Publishers' Catalogues.
[http://www.lights.ca/publisher]
[A worldwide directory of publishers' web pages for licensing and other purposes.]

WATCH: Writers, Artists and Their Copyright Holders.
[http://tyler.hrc.utexas.edu/]
[The WATCH website is maintained by the Harry Ransom Humanities Research Center at the University of Texas at Austin and the University of Reading to help users locate copyright holders and to provide basic information about U.S. Copyright Law to researchers.]

XanEdu.
[http://www.xanedu.com]
[XanEdu, formally Campus Custom Publishing, Inc., serves educational institutions and faculties' needs for compiling course-specific anthologies and other course materials through custom publishing services including clearing copyrights, paying royalties and securing copyright permissions where necessary. XanEdu provides custom publishing services through its content distributing agreement w/ProQuest Information and Learning which provides access to a large digital commercial archive including works of 8,000 publishers worldwide including periodicals, newspapers, out-of-

print books, dissertations and scholarly collections of manuscripts.]

ListServs

CNI-COPYRIGHT ListServ.
[http://www.cni.org/Hforums/cni-copyright/]
[An Internet discussion list on copyright and intellectual property related issues, with discussion among diverse contributors who may have expertise on copyright or who are seeking answers to their questions, sponsored by the Coalition for Networked Information.

LibLicense ListServ. Website and Listserv.
[http://www.library.yale.edu/~llicense/index.shtml]
[Licensing Electronic Resources, an Internet discussion list on library licensing issues and electronic content licensing for academic and research libraries, sponsored by Yale Univ. Lib., Commission on Preservation & Access, and Council on Library and Information Resources; includes sample license language and commentary.]

U.S. Copyright Office NEWSNET List Serv.
[http://www.copyright.gov/newsnet]
[An electronic mailing list from the U.S. Copyright Office that sends periodic e-mail messages, which alert subscribers to congressional and other hearings, new regulations, publications and other copyright-related subjects.]

OTHER SOURCES (from CENDI Copyright Task Group)

American Association for the Advancement of Science. *Electronic Publishing in Science: Seizing the Moment: Scientists' Authorship Rights in the Digital Age.*
[
http://www.aaas.org/spp/sfrl/projects/epub/finalrept.html
]
[This AAAS project examines intellectual property issues associated with electronic publishing in science.]

Cederqvist, Fredrik. *Copyright of Government Works: An International Survey*. New York Law School. [http://www.nyls.edu/cmc/papers/copyrite.txt] [Lists countries that do and do not copyright government works.]
Ebbinghouse, Carol. "Not All Laws Are Free: The Importance of the Veeck Case". *Searcher*, Vol. 10, No.2, Feb 2002. [<http://www.infotoday.com/searcher/feb02/ebbinghouse.htm]
Fishman, Stephen. *The Public Domain: How to Find & Use Copyright Free Writings, Music, Art & More*. Nolo Press. 2000. See [http://www.nolo.com/chapter/PUBL/PUBL_store_ch1_e.html] ["Chapter 1: Introduction to the Public Domain: Documenting Your Use of Public Domain Materials"]
Gellman, Robert. *Twin Evils: Government Copyright and Copyright-like Controls Over Government Information*. Syracuse Law Review v. 45('95) p. 999-1072. ADA394923
See [http://handle.dtic.mil/100.2/ADA394923]
ICSU/CODATA Summary of Database Protection Activities. [http://www.codata.org/data_access/summary.html]
International Standards Organization. *ISO Technical Report 21449. "Content Delivery and Rights Management - Functional Requirements for Identifiers and Descriptors for Use in the Music, Film, Video, Sound Recording, and Publishing Industries"* [http://www.nlc-bnc.ca/iso/tc46sc9/21449.htm] [Establishes a frame of reference for describing the nature of the business and information transactions that take place in the course of production, distribution, and rights management. It focuses specifically on the requirements of the originators, producers, distributors, registration authorities, and rights administrators involved in the development and delivery of intellectual and artistic content in an attempt to define relationships

to facilitate digital rights management in an e-commerce environment.]
Library of Congress. Federal Library and Information Center Committee (FLICC). *Copyright, Electronic Works, And Federal Libraries: Maintaining Equilibrium*. 1999 FLICC Forum on Federal Information Policies: A Summary of Proceedings, March 10, 1999-Library of Congress-Washington DC.
[http://lcweb.loc.gov/flicc/forum99.html]
[See "Providing Guidance-An Agency Policy on Copyright" by John Raubitschek, Patent Counsel-Department of Commerce
http://lcweb.loc.gov/flicc/forum99.html#Raubitschek]
Kim, Yong-Chan. *Copyright and Internet Social Claims and Government's Intervention*.
[http://www.msu.edu/user/kimyong2/copy.htm]
Levitt, David S. "Copyright Protection for U.S. Government Computer Programs". *IDEA: The Journal of Law and Technology.* 40 IDEA 225 (2000), Franklin Pierce Law Center.
[http://www.ipmall.org/hosted_resources/IDEA/40_IDEA/40-2_IDEA_225_Levitt.pdf]

Manz, Paul C., et al. "Protecting Government Works: The Copyright Issue. *Acquisition Review Quarterly*. Winter 2002. Defense Acquisition University, Ft. Belvoir, VA.
[http://www.dau.mil/pubs/arq/2002arq/Manz.pdf]
[The federal government, through its employees and contractors, produces commercially valuable inventions and information every day, often without any protection of the intellectual property involved. Intellectual property protection may provide sufficient incentive to investors to commercialize by granting a measure of exclusivity for a period of time. Federal program managers and directors, as well as private sector investors, should become familiar with all available intellectual property protection, such as: copyright law, including its impact on "government works," those created by federal and

contract employees; the alternatives that would permit the Government to own the copyright in "government works"; the ability to allow private sector companies to assign co-authored works; and the importance to a federal technology manager of such protection.]
Mitchell, Bradley W. *Works of the United States Government: Time to Consider Copyright Protection*. Thesis. Washington, D.C. George Washington University School of Law. 2002. ADA406618 [http://handle.dtic.mil/100.2/ADA406618]
[Includes a list of foreign national policies on copyright in government works and another of the policies of the 50 U.S. States.]
Modern Language Association. *MLA Position Statements and FAQs*. [http://www.mlanet.org/government/positions/]
Nash, Ralph C. and Rawicz, Leonard. *Intellectual Property in Government Contracts*. Fourth Edition. Vols. 1-3. Washington D.C., The George Washington University, School of Law, 1999. [Vol 1: Intellectual Property Rights; Vol 2: Technical Data Rights; Vol 3: Computer Software, Information, and Contract Remedies.]
National Research Council. Committee on Issues in the Transborder Flow of Scientific Data. *Bits of Power: Issues in Global Access to Scientific Data*. 1997 [http://books.nap.edu/catalog/5504.html]
[Chapter 4: Data from Publicly Funded Research-The Economic Perspective. Chapter 5: The Trend Toward Strengthened Intellectual Property Rights: A Potential Threat to Public-Good Uses of Scientific Data]
National Research Council. Office of International Affairs. *Global Dimensions of Intellectual Property Rights in Science and Technology*. 1993. [http://www.nap.edu/books/0309048338/html/index.html]
National Research Council. Commission on Physical Sciences, Mathematics and Applications. *Proceedings of the Workshop on Promoting Access to Scientific and*

Technical Data for the Public Interest: An Assessment of Policy Options. 1999.
[http://www.nap.edu/books/NI000903/html/]
National Research Council. Commission on Physical Sciences, Mathematics and Application. *A Question of Balance: Private Rights and the Public Interest in Scientific and Technical Databases*. 1999.
[http://www.nap.edu/books/0309068258/html/]
Nimmer, Melville B. and David Nimmer. *Nimmer on Copyright*. 5 vols. New York: Matthew Bender, 1992 (with periodic supplements)

Ockerbloom, John Mark, Editor. *The Online Books Page: Copyright and Related Issues*.
[http://digital.library.upenn.edu/books/okbooks.html]
[Sections address public domain, permissions, and duration of copyright in the U.S. and abroad]
How do I find out whether the book is in the public domain?
[http://digital.library.upenn.edu/books/okbooks.html#whatpd]
A Possible Exception for the Pre-1923 Public Domain Rule
[http://digital.library.upenn.edu/books/c-fineprint.html]
Okerson, Ann. *Who Owns Digital Works?: Computer Networks Challenge Copyright Law, But Some Proposed Cures May Be as Bad as the Disease*. Scientific American
[http://www.library.yale.edu/~okerson/sciam.html]
Price, Brian R. *Copyright in Government Publications: Historical Background, Judicial Interpretation, and Legislative Clarification*. Military Law Review, Vol. 74: 19-65, Fall 1976. ADA392794
[http://handle.dtic.mil/100.2/ADA392794]
Tresansky, John O. Copyright in Government Employee Authored Works. 30 Catholic Law Revue. 605 (1981). ADA392914
[http://handle.dtic.mil/100.2/ADA392914]

United Nations Educational, Scientific and Cultural Organization (UNESCO). *Copyright Laws and Treaties of the World*, 28th Supplement. Washington DC., BNA, Inc. 2000.
[Intellectual property laws of 200 countries and 16 international conventions.]
See also National Copyright Legislation
[http://www.unesco.org/culture/copy/]
U.S. National Commission on Libraries and Information Science. *Comprehensive Assessment of Public Information Dissemination June 2000* - March 2001
[http://www.nclis.gov/govt/assess/assess.html]
U.S. National Commission on Libraries and Information Science. *Report on the Assessment of Electronic Government Information Products. Commissioned by the U.S. Government Printing Office, Superintendent of Documents. March 30, 1999. Executive Summary -- Key Findings.*
[Product Characteristics. 10. Fifteen percent of the products surveyed are not in the public domain, for all or part of the product (table 27, p. 45). In addition, user fees are charged for 30 percent of the products (table 24, p. 43).]
[http://www.access.gpo.gov/su_docs/nclisassessment/report.html]

GOVERNMENT AGENCY POLICIES—A Sampling

Congressional Budget Office. *Privacy, Copyright, and Use Policies for the Web Site.*
[http://www.cbo.gov/Privacy.shtml]

Government Printing Office. *Public Domain / Copyright Notice.*
[http://www.gpoaccess.gov/about/legal.html]

Library of Congress. *Legal Notices: About Copyright and Collections.*
[http://www.loc.gov/homepage/legal.html]

National Air and Space Administration (NASA). Scientific and Technical Information. *NASA Privacy and Copyright Notice*.
[http://www.sti.nasa.gov/disclaimer.html]
Documentation, Approval, and Dissemination of NASA Scientific and Technical Information (NPG 2200.2A, September 3, 1997).
[http://nodis3.gsfc.nasa.gov/displayDir.cfm?Internal_ID=N_PG_2200_002A_&page_name=main]
NPR 2200.2A Requirements for Documentation, Approval, and Dissemination of NASA Scientific and Technical Information (STI) w/Change 1 (9/10/03).
[http://nodis3.gsfc.nasa.gov/displayDir.cfm?Internal_ID=N_PR_2200_002A_&page_name=main]
Restricted Distribution Types: Copyright [http://grcpublishing.grc.nasa.gov/techinfo/restrict.CFM]

National Archives and Records Agency (NARA)
Terms and Conditions for Using Our Web Site. Copyright, Restrictions, and Permissions Notice
[http://www.archives.gov/global_pages/privacy_and_use.html]

National Science Foundation. *Guidelines for Reproducing or Using Graphics from the NSF Web Site*.
[http://www.nsf.gov/policies/reuse.jsp]

U.S. Department of Agriculture
152.1-ARS. Procedures for Publishing Manuscripts and Abstracts with Non-USDA Publishers (Outside Publishing) March 10, 1998
[http://www.afm.ars.usda.gov/ppweb/152-01.pdf]
National Agriculture Library (NAL). *NAL Copyright Statement*.
[http://riley.nal.usda.gov/nal_display/index.php?info_center=8&tax_level=1&tax_subject=489#NAL%20Copyright%20Statement]

U.S. Department of Commerce

Department of Commerce. *Administrative Order DAO 219-1: Public Communications* [http://204.193.232.34/cgi-bin/doit.cgi?204:112:d27ddcc65cae3134b8bf1b865dbd576aae631885580a96f24b4e675af66a10fb:267]

National Institute of Standards and Technology (NIST). *Disclaimer. Use of NIST Information.* [http://www.nist.gov/public_affairs/disclaim.htm]

U.S. Department of Defense

Office of the Assistant Secretary of Defense (Public Affairs). *Defenselink: DoD Webmasters Policies And Guidelines.* [http://www.defenselink.mil/webmasters/]

Defense Information Systems Agency. (DISA) Defense Technical Information Center.

DTIC Scientific & Technical Documents Selection Criteria: Copyright. [http://www.dtic.mil/dtic/submitting/selec_criteria.html#Copyright]

DTIC Guidelines for Determining Copyright. [http://www.dtic.mil/dtic/submitting/copyright.html]

Office of the Under Secretary of Defense (Acquisitions & Technology). Office of Acquisition Initiatives. *Intellectual Property: Navigating Through Commercial Waters (Version 1.1)*, October 2001. [http://www.acq.osd.mil/dpap/Docs/intelprop.pdf]

Office of the Assistant Secretary of Defense (Command, Control, Communications & Intelligence) *WEB SITE ADMINISTRATION. Part II - Process and Procedures. November 25, 1998. INFORMATION POSTING PROCESS 3.5 Content Review 3.5.5. Copyrighted Material.* Copyrighted material will be used only when allowed by prevailing copyright laws and may be used only if the materials relate to the Component's mission. Consult with Counsel when using any copyrighted material. [http://www.defenselink.mil/webmasters/policy/dod_web

_policy_12071998_with_amendments_and_corrections.html#part2]
U.S. Air Force Museum. *Privacy, Security and Use Notice*.
[http://www.nationalmuseum.af.mil/main/disclaimer.asp]
U.S. Army. Army Regulation 25-30. 2 June 2004. *The Army Publishing and Printing Program. See Chapter 2: Publications, Section I: Statutory Restrictions and Official Publications and Section V: Copyright*.
[http://www.usapa.army.mil/pdffiles/r25_30.pdf]

U.S. Department of Education
ERIC Database Use Policy
[
http://www.eric.ed.gov/ERICWebPortal/resources/html/help/help_popup_privacy.html]

U.S. Department of Energy
Energy Information Administration. *Copyright Information*.
[http://www.eia.doe.gov/neic/aboutEIA/copy_right.html]
Fermilab. Information Resources Department. *Policy for Execution of Copyright Transfer and Agreement Forms*.
[http://bss.fnal.gov/techpubs/copyrtinfo.html]
Fermilab. *DOE Disclaimers and Copyright Notices*.
[http://www.fnal.gov/pub/disclaim.html]
Lawrence Livermore National Laboratory (LLNL). *Notice to Users. Copyright Status.*
[http://www.llnl.gov/disclaimer.html]
Los Alamos National Laboratory (LANL). *Copyright Notice for Scientific and Technical Information Only*.
[http://www.lanl.gov/misc/copyright.html]
Office of Scientific and Technical Information (OSTI). *Technical Information Management Program (TIMP.)*
[http://www.osti.gov/timp.html]

U.S. Department of Health and Human Services

Agency for Healthcare Research and Quality. *Guideline User Policies for Electronic Versions. Copyright*. [http://www.ahcpr.gov/news/gdluser.htm#copyright]
Federal Drug Administration (FDA). *Linking To or Copying Information On the FDA Website* [http://www.fda.gov/copyright.html]
National Institutes of Health Libraries. *Disclaimers - Copyright Restrictions Applicable to NIH Staff* [http://nihlibrary.nih.gov/Disclaimers.htm]
National Library of Medicine (NLM) *Copyright Information*. [http://www.nlm.nih.gov/copyright.html]
National Library of Medicine. (NLM) *Policy on Acquiring Copyrighted Material in Electronic Format*. April 27, 2000.
[http://www.nlm.nih.gov/pubs/acqcopyrightmat.html]
National Library of Medicine (NLM). *Agreement for the Use of Images from Visible Human Data Set*. [http://www.nlm.nih.gov/research/visible/vhpagree.txt]
National Library of Medicine (NLM). *License Agreement for Use of the UMLS® Metathesaurus®* [http://www.nlm.nih.gov/research/umls/license.html]
National Library of Medicine (NLM). *Fact Sheet: National Library of Medicine Trademarks*. [http://www.nlm.nih.gov/pubs/factsheets/trademarks.html]
National Library of Medicine (NLM). *Profiles in Science FAQ 5. May I have permission to use the documents (letters, articles, photographs, etc.) from Profiles in Science?*
[http://profiles.nlm.nih.gov/Help/FAQ/#permission]

U.S. Department of Interior
U.S. Geological Survey. (USGS) *USGS Privacy Policy and Disclaimers. Copyright*. [http://www.usgs.gov/privacy.html#copyright]

U.S. Department of Justice. Computer Crime & Intellectual Property Section, Criminal Division

Federal Prosecution of Violations of Intellectual Property Rights (Copyrights, Trademarks and Trade Secrets). May 1997. Washington, D.C.
[http://www.usdoj.gov/criminal/cybercrime/CFAleghist.htm]
DOJ Criminal Resource Manual. *1854 Copyright Infringement -- First Sale Doctrine*.
[http://www.usdoj.gov:80/usao/eousa/foia_reading_room/usam/title9/crm01854.htm]
Protecting Intellectual Property Rights: Copyrights, Trademarks and Trade Secrets
[http://www.usdoj.gov:80/criminal/cybercrime/ip.html]

www.cybercrime.gov
[http://www.usdoj.gov:80/criminal/cybercrime/index.html]

Copyrighted Materials and the FOIA, FOIA Update, Vol. IV, No. 4, Fall 1983, OIP Guidance
[http://www.usdoj.gov:80/oip/foia_updates/Vol_IV_4/page3.htm]
[In sum, agencies should carefully examine all copyrighted materials encompassed within FOIA requests to determine whether they qualify for Exemption 4 protection. As for those copyrighted materials to which Exemption 4 is inapplicable, the position of the Department of Justice is that the release of such materials under the FOIA is a defensible "fair use."]

Memorandum for Andrew J. Pincus, General Counsel, Department of Commerce From Randolph D. Moss, Acting Assistant Attorney Opinion: *RE: Whether Government Reproduction of Copyrighted Materials Invariably is a "Fair Use" under Section 107 of the Copyright Act of 1976*. April 30, 1999.
[http://lcweb.loc.gov/flicc/gc/fairuse.html]

U.S. Mint. *Privacy Policy & Terms of Use. Intellectual Property.*
[http://www.usmint.gov/policy/index.cfm?action=TermsOfUse]

U.S. Patent & Trademark Office (USPTO). *Editorial Standards. Copyright and Trademark Issues RE: Materials from USPTO Website*. Also see Terms of Use.
[http://www.uspto.gov/main/ccpubguide.htm]

U.S. Senate. *Photo Collection of the Senate Historical Office: Copyright Information for the Collection*
[http://www.senate.gov/artandhistory/history/common/generic/Photo_Collection_of_the_Senate_Historical_Office.htm]

PUBLISHER COPYRIGHT TRANSFER AGREEMENTS—A sampling

American Association for Artificial Intelligence. AAAI Press Copyright Form
[http://www.aaai.org/Press/Author/copyrightform.pdf]
American Geophysical Union. Copyright Agreement
[http://www.agu.org/pubs/Copyrght.pdf]
American Physical Society. Transfer of Copyright Agreement.
[http://forms.aps.org/author/copytrnsfr.pdf]
Association for Computing Machinery. ACM Copyright Form
[http://www.acm.org/pubs/copyright_form.html]

Elsevier Author Gateway.
[http://authors.elsevier.com/]

Note: Under ***Publisher Information***, choose *Getting Published with Elsevier Science*. Under ***After Acceptance***, choose Copyright Information. Elsevier does not post its Copyright Transfer Agreement nor does the information presented on the Author Gateway mention Government or Government-contracted works.

IEEE Computer Society. Copyright Form Information. [http://www.computer.org/portal/web/publications/copyright]
IEEE Copyright Form [http://www.ieee.org/publications_standards/publications/rights/copyrightmain.html]
BioMedical Library Association. BMLA. Notice to Authors [http://www.mlanet.org/publications/jmla/jmlainfo.html#note]
Materials Research Society. Instructions for Authors. Copyright Transfer. [http://www.mrs.org/publications/books/manuscript_info/proc_copyright_info.pdf]
Science Publishers [http://www.sciencekomm.at/publish.html]

References

[1]Berne Convention http://www.copyright.gov/title17/92appii.html
[2]17 USC § 106 http://www.copyright.gov/title17/92chap1.html#106
[3]Digital Millennium Copyright Act http://www.copyright.gov/legislation/hr2281.pdf
[4]17 USC § 1202(c) http://www.copyright.gov/title17/92chap12.html#1202
[5]17 USC § 107 http://www.copyright.gov/title17/92chap1.html#107
[6]Federal Acquisition Regulation http://www.arnet.gov/far/
[7]17 USC § 202 http://www.copyright.gov/title17/92chap2.html#202
[8]17 USC § 109 http://www.copyright.gov/title17/92chap1.html#109
[9]OMB Circular A-130 http://www.whitehouse.gov/omb/circulars/a130/a130.html
[10]Freedom of Information Act http://www.usdoj.gov/oip/foi-act.htm
[11]Privacy Act http://www.accessreports.com/statutes/PA.htm

[12]44 U.S.C. § 1901
http://www.access.gpo.gov/uscode/title44/chapter19_.html
[13]44 U.S.C. § 3301
http://www.access.gpo.gov/uscode/title44/title44.html
[14]17 USC § 101, Definitions
http://www.copyright.gov/title17/92chap1.html#101
[15]17 USC § 101, Definitions
http://www.copyright.gov/title17/92chap1.html#101
[16]17 USC § 201(a)
http://www.copyright.gov/title17/92chap2.html#201
[17]License Agreement for Use of the UMLS® Metathesaurus®
http://www.nlm.nih.gov/research/umls/license.html
[18]17 USC § 101, Definitions
http://www.copyright.gov/title17/92chap1.html#101
[19]17 USC § 201(d)
http://www.copyright.gov/title17/92chap2.html#201
[20]17 USC § 204
http://www.copyright.gov/title17/92chap2.html#204
[21]Title 17 of the United States Code (17 USC - Copyrights
http://www.copyright.gov/title17/92chap2.html#204
[22]Title 37 Code of Federal Regulations
http://www.access.gpo.gov/nara/cfr/waisidx_99/37cfrv1_99.html#201
[23]U.S. Constitution, Article 1, Section 8
http://www.archives.gov/exhibits/charters/constitution_transcript.html
[24]Berne Convention
http://www.copyright.gov/title17/92appii.html
[25]Sonny Bono Copyright Term Extension Act
http://www.copyright.gov/legislation/s505.pdf
[26]Digital Millennium Copyright Act
http://www.copyright.gov/legislation/hr2281.pdf
[27]17 USC § 106
http://www.copyright.gov/title17/92chap1.html#106
[28]17 USC § 106 A
http://www.copyright.gov/title17/92chap1.html#106A
[29]Circular 101: Copyright Basics
http://www.copyright.gov/circs/circ1.html
[30]Circular 40, Copyright Registration for Works of the Visual

Arts http://www.copyright.gov/circs/circ1.html
[31]The U.S. Copyright Law, Chapter 3 -- Duration of Copyright http://www.copyright.gov/title17/92chap3.html
[32]Information Circular 15a - Duration of Copyright: Provisions of the Law Dealing with the Length of Copyright Protection http://www.copyright.gov/circs/circ15a.pdf
[33]Fact sheet FL 15 - New Terms for Copyright Protection http://www.copyright.gov/fls/sl15.html
[34]When Works Pass Into the Public Domain http://www.unc.edu/~unclng/public-d.htm
[34a]Copyright Term and the Public Domain in the United States http://www.copyright.cornell.edu/training/Hirtle_Public_Domain.htm
[35]17 USC §§ 107 through 120 http://www.copyright.gov/title17/92chap1.html
[36]17 USC § 107 http://www.copyright.gov/title17/92chap1.html#107
[37]17 USC § 107 http://www.copyright.gov/title17/92chap1.html#107
[38]National Library of Medicine http://www.nlm.nih.gov/disclaimer.html
[39]NASA Center for AeroSpace Information (CASI) http://www.sti.nasa.gov/disclaimer.html
[40]Library of Congress http://www.loc.gov/homepage/legal.html#COPY
[41]17 USC § 204 http://www.copyright.gov/title17/92chap2.html#204
[42]Copyright Office Circular 22 http://www.copyright.gov/circs/circ22.html
[43]Library of Congress Information System http://www.loc.gov/catalog/locisint.html
[44]Washington Post http://www.washingtonpost.com/wp-srv/interact/longterm/talk/copy.htm
[45]New York Times http://www.time.com/time/faq/#link
[46]Pub. L. No 105-304, 112 Stat. 2860 http://www.copyright.gov/legislation/hr2281.pdf
[47]17 U.S.C § 1201 et al. http://www.copyright.gov/title17/92chap12.html#1201
[48]17 U.S.C. § 1201(a)(1)

http://www.copyright.gov/title17/92chap12.html#1201
[49]17 U.S.C. § 1201(a)(1)
http://www.copyright.gov/title17/92chap12.html#1201
[50]17 U.S.C. § 1202
http://www.copyright.gov/title17/92chap12.html#1202
[51]17 U.S.C. § 512
http://www.copyright.gov/title17/92chap5.html#512
[52]U.S. Copyright Office Summary of the DMCA.
http://www.copyright.gov/legislation/dmca.pdf
[53]Patents
http://www.uspto.gov/web/offices/pac/doc/general/whatis.htm
[54]Trademarks
http://www.uspto.gov/web/offices/tac/tmfaq.htm#
[55]U.S. Patent and Trademark Office http://www.uspto.gov/
[56]17 USC § 101, Definitions
http://www.copyright.gov/title17/92chap1.html#101
[57]Copyright in Government Employee Authored Works
http://stinet.dtic.mil/cgi-bin/fulcrum_main.pl?database=TR_U2&numrecords=25&search.DOC_TEXT=ADA392914
[58]Public Affairs Associate V. Rickover
http://caselaw.lp.findlaw.com/scripts/getcase.pl?court=US&vol=369&invol=111
[59]17 USC § 105
http://www.copyright.gov/title17/92chap1.html#105
[60]USC §105 http://www.copyright.gov/title17/92chap1.html
[61]Gellman http://stinet.dtic.mil/
[62]Pfeiffer v. Central Intelligence Agency
http://www.ll.georgetown.edu/federal/judicial/dc/opinions/94opinions/94-5107a.html"
[63]OMB Circular A-130
http://www.whitehouse.gov/omb/circulars/a130/a130.html
[64]Department of Defense Directive 5230.9
http://stinet.dtic.mil/stinfo/data/DoDD_52309.pdf
[65]DOD Instruction 5230.29
http://www.dtic.mil/whs/directives/corres/pdf/523029p.pdf
[66]statutes
http://www.defenselink.mil/pubs/foi/98report/CONTENTS.html#ItemIV

[67]CRADA http://www.usbr.gov/research/tech-transfer/together/crada/whatcrada.html
[68]NASA Space Act Agreements http://www.hq.nasa.gov/ogc/samanual.html
[69]Terms and Conditions for the Visible Human Project http://www.nlm.nih.gov/research/visible/getting_data.html
[70]License Agreement for Use of the UMLS® Metathesaurus® http://wwwcf.nlm.nih.gov/umlslicense/snomed/license.cfm
[71]17 USC §105 http://www.copyright.gov/title17/92chap1.html#105
[72]17 USC § 403 http://www.copyright.gov/title17/92chap4.html#403
[73]Matthew Bender & Co. v. West PublishingCo.http://www.kentlaw.edu/classes/rwarner/legalaspects_ukraine/copyright/cases/bender_v_west.html
[74]IEEE Copyright Form http://www.ieee.org/publications_standards/publications/rights/copyrightmain.html
[75]Kluwer Academic/Plenum Publishing Transfer of Copyright Form http://www.bga.org/journal/Kluwer-Plenum_copyright.pdf
[76]17 USC § 101, Definitions http://www.copyright.gov/title17/92chap1.html#101
[77]17 USC § 201 http://www.copyright.gov/title17/92chap2.html#201
[78]Federal Acquisition Regulations http://www.arnet.gov/far/
[79]FAR Subpart 27.4--Rights in Data and Copyrights http://www.arnet.gov/far/current/html/Subpart%2027_4.html
[80]FAR general data rights clause, 52.227-14 http://www.arnet.gov/far/current/html/52_227.html#1109286
[81]Defense Federal Acquisition Regulation Supplement (DFARS) Subpart 227.4 http://www.acq.osd.mil/dpap/dars/dfars/html/current/227_4.htm
[82]Part 211 http://www.acq.osd.mil/dpap/dars/dfars/html/current/211_0.htm
[83]DFARS Part 252 http://www.acq.osd.mil/dpap/dars/dfars/html/current/252_1.htm

[84] DFARS Part 227.4
http://www.acq.osd.mil/dpap/dars/dfars/html/current/227_4.htm
[85]FAR 27.400
http://www.arnet.gov/far/current/html/Subpart%2027_4.html
[86]DFARS 227.7103-9
http://www.acq.osd.mil/dpap/dars/dfars/html/current/227_71.htm#227.7103-9
[87]DFARS 252.227-7013-4
http://www.acq.osd.mil/dpap/dars/dfars/html/current/252227.htm#252.227-7013
[88]DFARS 252.227-7020
http://www.acq.osd.mil/dpap/dars/dfars/html/current/252227.htm#252.227-7020
[89]FAR 52.227-20
http://farsite.hill.af.mil/reghtml/regs/far2afmcfars/fardfars/far/52_227.htm#P495_117738
[90]DFARS 227.7103-9
http://www.acq.osd.mil/dpap/dars/dfars/html/current/227_71.htm#227.7103-9
[91]DFARS 227.7203-9
http://www.acq.osd.mil/dpap/dars/dfars/html/current/227_72.htm#227.7203-9
[92]FAR 52.227-14
http://farsite.hill.af.mil/reghtml/regs/far2afmcfars/fardfars/far/52_227.htm#P328_81380
[93]FAR 27.404(f)(2)
http://www.arnet.gov/far/current/html/Subpart%2027_4.html
[94]DFARS 227.7103-9(a)(2)
http://www.acq.osd.mil/dpap/dars/dfars/html/current/227_71.htm#227.7103-9
[95]FAR special works data rights clause, 52.227-17
http://farsite.hill.af.mil/reghtml/regs/far2afmcfars/fardfars/far/52_227.htm#P444_107388
[96]FAR 27.404(g)(3)
http://www.arnet.gov/far/current/html/Subpart%2027_4.html
[97]NASA FAR Supplement
http://www.hq.nasa.gov/office/procurement/regs/5227.htm
[98]DFARS 252.227-7020

http://www.acq.osd.mil/dpap/dars/dfars/html/current/252227.htm#252.227-7020
[99]FAR general data rights clause, 52.227-14
http://www.acqnet.gov/far/current/html/52_227.html
[100]FAR 27.404(g)
http://www.acqnet.gov/far/current/html/Subpart%2027_4.html#wp1041836
[101]FAR special works data rights clause, 52.227-14(d)
http://www.acqnet.gov/far/current/html/52_227.html
[102]FAR special works data rights clause
http://www.acqnet.gov/far/current/html/52_227.html
[103]DFARS clause 252.227-7013
http://www.acq.osd.mil/dpap/dars/dfars/html/current/252227.htm#252.227-7013
[104]DFARS clause 252.227-7020
http://www.acq.osd.mil/dpap/dars/dfars/html/current/252227.htm#252.227-7020
[105]DFARS 227.7106(b)
http://www.acq.osd.mil/dpap/dars/dfars/html/current/227_71.htm#227.7106
[106]FAR 27.404(f)(1)(v)
http://farsite.hill.af.mil/reghtml/regs/far2afmcfars/fardfars/far/52_227.htm#P326_97762
[107]DFARS clause 252.227-7013(f)
http://www.acq.osd.mil/dpap/dars/dfars/html/current/252227.htm#252.227-7013
and 252.227-7014(f)
http://www.acq.osd.mil/dpap/dars/dfars/html/current/252227.htm#252.227-7014
[108]OMB Circular A-110 Uniform Administrative Requirements for Grants and Agreements With Institutions of Higher Education, Hospitals, and Other Non-Profit Organizations
http://www.whitehouse.gov/omb/circulars/a110/a110.html
[109]OMB Circular A-102, Grants and Cooperative Agreements with State and Local Governments
http://www.whitehouse.gov/omb/circulars/a102/a102.html
[110]Section 36 of Circular A-110
http://www.whitehouse.gov/omb/circulars/a110/a110.html#36
[111]new requirements for providing government access

http://www.whitehouse.gov/omb/fedreg/a110-finalnotice.html
[112]Section 36 of Circular A-110(a)
http://www.whitehouse.gov/omb/circulars/a110/a110.html#36
[113]FAR Clause 52.227.14
http://farsite.hill.af.mil/reghtml/regs/far2afmcfars/fardfars/far/52_227.htm#P248_51622
[114]27.409(a)
http://farsite.hill.af.mil/reghtml/regs/far2afmcfars/fardfars/far/27.htm#P420_100140
[115]Policy on Enhancing Public Access to Archived Publications Resulting from NIH-Funded Research
http://www.nih.gov/about/publicaccess/
[116]PubMed Central http://www.pubmedcentral.nih.gov/
[117]28 USC § 1498 (b)
http://www4.law.cornell.edu/uscode/html/uscode28/usc_sec_28_00001498----000-.html
[118]John C. Boyle v. United States
http://www.ll.georgetown.edu/federal/judicial/fed/opinions/99opinions/99-5125.html
[119]U.S. Department of Justice opinion
http://lcweb.loc.gov/flicc/gc/fairuse.html
[120]"Application of the Copyright Doctrine of Fair Use to the Reproduction of Copyrighted Material for Intelligence Purposes"
http://handle.dtic.mil/100.2/ADA389801
[121]Copyright Office Circular 1 http://www.copyright.gov/circs/
[122]17 USC § 107
http://www.copyright.gov/title17/92chap1.html#107
[123]17 USC § 108
http://www.copyright.gov/title17/92chap1.html#108
[124]CONTU Guidelines on Photocopying under Interlibrary Loan Arrangements
http://www.cni.org/docs/infopols/CONTU.html
[125]Copyright Office Circular 21
http://www.copyright.gov/circs/circ21.pdf
[126]17 USC § 108
http://www.copyright.gov/title17/92chap1.html#108
[127]17 USC § 107
http://www.copyright.gov/title17/92chap1.html#107

[128]17 USC § 108
http://www.copyright.gov/title17/92chap1.html#108
[129] Licensing Electronic Publications for Use in a Federal Agency http://lcweb.loc.gov/flicc/video/licen/licen.html
[130]License Agreements for Electronic Products and Services: Frequently Asked Questions
http://www.cendi.gov/publications/01-3lic_agree.html
[131]Policy on Acquiring Copyrighted Material in Electronic Format http://www.nlm.nih.gov/pubs/acqcopyrightmat.html
[132]Library Use and Disclaimer Notice
http://infoweb2.nrl.navy.mil/index.cfm?i=90
[133]Permissions: Using Digital Materials from the Smithsonian Institution Libraries http://www.sil.si.edu/permissions/
[134]sample letter requesting permission
http://www.utsystem.edu:80/ogc/intellectualproperty/permmm.htm
[135]28 USC § 1498 (b)
http://www4.law.cornell.edu/uscode/html/uscode28/usc_sec_28_00001498----000-.html
[136]17 USC § 110
http://www.copyright.gov/title17/92chap1.html#110
[137]17 U.S.C. § 106(4)
http://www.copyright.gov/title17/92chap1.html#106
[138]17 USC § 101
http://www.copyright.gov/title17/92chap1.html#101
[139]H.R. Rep. No.94-1476
http://en.wikisource.org/wiki/Copyright_Law_Revision_(House_Report_No._94-1476)/Annotated
[140]Patry, William F. Patry on Copyright. St. Paul, MN: Thomson West (Westlaw), 2008
[141]Columbia Pictures Industries, Inc. v. Redd Horne Inc
http://www.law.cornell.edu/copyright/cases/749_F2d_154.htm
[142]17 U.S.C. § 106
http://www.copyright.gov/title17/92chap1.html#106
[143]17 USC § 107
http://www.copyright.gov/title17/92chap1.html#107
[144]17 USC § 110(1)
http://www.copyright.gov/title17/92chap1.html#110
[145]17 USC § 110(4)

http://www.copyright.gov/title17/92chap1.html#110
[146]17 USC § 107
http://www.copyright.gov/title17/92chap1.html#107
[147]17 USC § 108
http://www.copyright.gov/title17/92chap1.html#108
[148]17 USC § 109
http://www.copyright.gov/title17/92chap1.html#109
[149]28 USC § 1498 (b)
http://www4.law.cornell.edu/uscode/html/uscode28/usc_sec_28_00001498----000-.html
[150]DFARS Subpart 227.70
http://www.acq.osd.mil/dpap/dars/dfars/html/current/227_70.htm
[151]28 USC § 1498 (b)
http://www4.law.cornell.edu/uscode/html/uscode28/usc_sec_28_00001498----000-.html

Chapter 5 - HOW TO READ A PUBLISHING AGREEMENT

Authors who publish through a publisher other than themselves will be subjected to a publishing agreement. This is a very important document and one that requires an author to seek legal counsel. Below is an article written by a copyright attorney that discusses in detail what a publishing agreement is all about.

By David Koehser, Attorney At Law

http://www.dklex.com/how-to-read-a-publishing-agreement.html

Publishing Agreements tend to be lengthy and complex documents, and publishers and authors usually benefit from obtaining legal advice rather than simply forging ahead on their own. However, even a publisher or author who elects to obtain legal advice can and should have a basic understanding of the key provisions found in a typical publishing agreement. Some of those provisions are discussed below:

Grant of Rights

Every publishing agreement will contain a grant of rights clause, by which the author grants certain exclusive rights to the publisher. These rights typically are divided into primary rights (the right to publish the book in all formats, including print and electronic) and subsidiary rights (other rights, such as the right to create and publish audio books, foreign language editions of the book, and adapted or condensed editions of the book; the right to grant others permission to publish excerpts from the book; the right to produce and distribute motion pictures or tv programs based on the book; and the right to produce and distribute merchandise based on the book or characters in the book).

Historically, publishers exercised primary rights and licensed subsidiary rights to third parties. However, the current trend is for publishers to acquire the right to exercise and license both the primary rights and the subsidiary rights.

A more logical approach to subsidiary rights is to determine which party is in a better position to market those rights. Authors are usually advised to retain as many subsidiary rights as possible. However, a more logical approach is often to determine which party is in a better position to market the various subsidiary rights in a work, and then let each party control those rights which it is most likely to exercise or for which it is most likely to find licenses. For example, unless an author is represented by an agent with strong foreign rights connections, it is unlikely that the author will have much luck licensing foreign rights to a single book. However, publishers typically have established licensing relationships with foreign publishers, and have the ability to package the author's book with several other books to secure foreign rights deals. On the other side of the table, an author may have a special connection with a television producer, playwright or other potential licensee, and, in those cases, the author should retain control over the specific subsidiary rights which the author is well positioned to license.

Delivery Obligations

The author needs to ensure that the date for delivery can be met. Authors by nature tend to be procrastinators, and thus the manuscript delivery clause of a publishing agreement can be critical. Most agreements will require the author to deliver a manuscript, acceptable to the publisher in content and form, by a specific date. The author needs to ensure that the date for delivery can be met. If there are any doubts in this regard, the author should ask that the date be extended prior to signing the agreement, as it can be difficult to get an extension after the agreement is in place.

The author should also get clarification from the publisher as to the required form for the manuscript, and as to the publisher's expectations as to content. From the publisher's perspective, courts have generally held that a publisher cannot reject a manuscript out of hand, and must work with the author to revise the manuscript to the publisher's satisfaction. Thus if the publisher finds the initial manuscript to be unacceptable, the publisher should be required to notify the author of its objections, and to give the author at least one opportunity to revise and resubmit the manuscript.

Editorial Changes

A publisher will typically want the right to make changes in an author's work, particularly if the author has never been published before, and an author will usually want his or her work to be published as written, or at least to have a right of approval over any changes made by the publisher. There is no right or wrong answer to this dilemma. Rather, it is up to the parties to reach an understanding, and to include that understanding in the agreement. A publisher who wants the unlimited right to make editorial changes or to change the title of the work should obtain that right in the publishing agreement. Conversely, an author who wants to control the editing of his or her work or set the title for the work should insist that the agreement require the author's approval before any changes can be made.

Publication Deadline

In most cases, an author will want to see his or her book get to market sooner rather than later. This generally holds true for the publisher as well, although publishers sometimes end up delaying publication dates due to other more pressing projects, staffing problems, cash flow considerations or for other reasons. Because of this, it is usually a good idea for an author to set an outside date for publication, and to have an option to regain the rights in the book if publication does not occur by that date. Having a publication deadline is also in the best interest of the publisher, as the publisher can pair that deadline with a liquidated damages provision. If the publisher fails to meet the deadline, the agreement will usually state that the author's only remedy for the publisher's failure to publish is to get back the rights in the book and to keep any advances that have been paid. This shields the publisher from any lawsuit for loss of royalties or other losses by the author arising out of the publisher's failure to publish.

Representations, Warranties and Indemnification

A publisher will always require the author to represent and warrant that the manuscript is original and has not been copied from another source. The publishing business is not without risks. For example, a person other than the author of a book may claim that he or she is the real author of the book, or a person identified in the book may claim that he or she has been defamed by statements made in the book. In order to protect against these risks, publishers typically require authors to make certain representations as to the material included in their books, and to shield the publisher against any losses in the event those representations prove to be untrue. An author is in the best position to know if the material included in that author's manuscript has been copied from another source, has been previously published, is subject to any other contract or claim, or was told to the author in confidence. Also, an author who is an expert on the subject addressed in the book should know if the information contained in the book is accurate and correct. Accordingly, a publisher will always require the author to represent and warrant that the manuscript is original and has not been copied from another source, that the author is the sole author of the manuscript, that the manuscript is not already under contract to another publisher or subject to any claims of creditors, former spouses or others, and that the publication of the book will not breach any obligation of confidentiality of the author. A publisher will also require the author to represent and warrant that the information contained in the manuscript is accurate or is based upon reasonable research.

In addition to requiring the author to verify information which the author should know, most publishers also require the author to make representations and warranties as to issues which are not as clear cut. For example, an author will usually be required to represent and warrant that the material in the manuscript will not defame any person or infringe on that person's right of privacy or publicity, will not be obscene, and will not result in injury to any reader. In many cases, the question of whether material is defamatory, obscene or infringes on any right of privacy or publicity is a legal question that can only be resolved by a court. Accordingly, an author may ask that the representations and warranties on these matters be only "to the best of the author's knowledge."

In all cases, an author should ensure that his or her representations and warranties apply only to the material provided by the author, and not extend to any material that was added by or changed at the request of the publisher.

Indemnification essentially means that the author agrees to become an insurance company for the publisher. The most significant part of the representations and warranties section of a publishing agreement is the author's promise of indemnification. Indemnification essentially means that the author agrees to become an insurance company for the publisher should any person sue the publisher based on a claim that the author's book infringes that person's copyright, defames that person, violates that person's right of privacy or publicity, or causes any other injury covered by the author's representations and warranties. The publisher typically has the right to hire its own attorneys (at the author's expense) to defend against these claims.

The indemnification clause in a publishing agreement obviously exposes the author to a great deal of risk, and should, at a minimum, cause the author to review carefully all material that he or she plans to include in the book. In addition, in some cases an author may be able to limit the potential liability under an indemnification clause by adding one or more of the following provisions to the agreement:

- The author and the publisher will split all defense costs equally if any claim covered by the author's representations and warranties is abandoned, or if a court dismisses the claim or rules in favor of the author and the publisher.
- The author's indemnification obligations will apply only to an actual breach of any of the author's representations and warranties, as determined by a court. In other words, the author will not be obligated to pay for the cost of defending against claims that are found to be without merit.
- The author will have the right to approve all settlements made by the publisher.
- The author will be added as an additional insured under the publisher's media perils insurance policy. Until recently, large publishers were generally willing to add an author under their insurance policies. However, this has become less and less common as insurance costs have risen. Many small publishers do not carry media perils insurance, and thus will react with total befuddlement if asked to add an author as an additional insured under their (nonexistent) policy. However, even if a publisher has insurance coverage and is willing to add an author under the policy, the author should not assume that he or she is home free. Most policies have large deductibles, and the author will usually remain liable on the author's indemnification promise up to the

amount of the deductible. In addition, many policies do not cover all of the possible claims that can arise out of the author's representations and warranties, and the author will remain liable for any claims not covered under the policy. Finally, a policy will provide coverage only up to the policy limits. If another book published by the publisher results in a multi-million dollar libel judgment, there may not be any coverage remaining for a subsequent claim arising out of the author's book.

The Money – Advances, Royalties, Payment and Accounting

Whether a publisher will or will not pay an advance for a book may depend on several factors, including the size of the publisher, the market into which the book will be sold, and the reputation of the author. If an advance is paid, it will usually be paid in two or three installments, with the first installment to be paid upon the signing of the publishing agreement, and subsequent installments to be paid upon delivery of a satisfactory manuscript and upon first publication. The advance should be nonrefundable, unless the author fails to deliver an acceptable manuscript by the due date in the agreement or any of the author's representations and warranties turn out to be untrue. Under some agreements, if the publisher rejects the manuscript as unsatisfactory, the author will only be obligated to repay the advance from the proceeds received under any other contract that the author enters into for the work.

Royalties may be calculated as percentage of the retail list price of each copy of the book sold, or as a percentage of the actual amount that the publisher receives from each copy sold. The former is more common with larger publishers, and the latter is more common with smaller publishers, and for books in certain markets, such as textbooks and children's books. The royalty rate, and, in some cases, the royalty base, will change depending on the type of sale. For example, the royalty for regular trade sales, at a discount of less than 55%, may be 10% of the retail price, but the royalty for sales at discounts of 55% or higher may be 10% of the net amounts received by the publisher.

In addition to royalties, an author will usually receive a share of the net amounts received by the publisher from licenses of any of the subsidiary rights in the book. For example, if the publisher grants a foreign language translation license to a German publisher and receives an advance of $5,000, the publisher will be obligated to share that advance with the author based on the formula in the publishing agreement. As a general rule, the publisher and the author share equally in proceeds from subsidiary rights licenses, but in some cases, either the author or the publisher may be entitled to a larger share.

Payments of royalties and shares of subsidiary rights licenses are usually made twice per year, although some publishers still adhere to a once per year payment schedule. Payments are usually made anywhere from 60 days to 120 days after the close of each accounting period. While a publisher's payment terms may seem somewhat slow from the perspective of an author, the publisher is not likely to change its terms for an individual author, and each author under contract with that publisher will be paid in accordance with the same terms.

Although it is rare for an author to audit a publisher's books, every publishing agreement should give the author the right to do so. Even if the author and the publisher have a relationship of complete trust, there is always the possibility that the publisher will later sell its business to another publisher with less honorable accounting practices. From a publisher's perspective, an audit clause can be useful in that it allows the publisher to define, and perhaps limit, the scope of an audit.

Revisions

Textbooks and other nonfiction works often need to be revised on a regular basis in order to remain saleable, and thus the publishing agreements for these books should provide for revisions. The author will typically have a right of first refusal to prepare any revised edition, although the author may lose this right if he or she declines to participate in a revision. Even if the author does not participate in a revision, the publisher will usually want the right to continue to use the author's name with any revised edition (although the author may want to retain the right to remove his or her name from a revised edition).

The royalty to be paid to a nonparticipating author for the first revised edition will usually be the same as the royalty for the first edition of the book, less any costs incurred by the publisher in retaining another author to prepare the revised edition, but that royalty will most likely be reduced for any subsequent revised editions in which the author does not participate. For example, the author may get the full royalty, less any amounts paid by the publisher to another author to prepare the revision, for the first revised edition, and may get 50% of that amount for the second revised edition, with no royalty payable after the second revised edition.

Option for Next Work

Most publishing agreements contain an option clause which gives the publisher the first right to publish the author's next book. Under a typical option clause, the author must submit the manuscript for the author's next work to the publisher before submitting it to any other publisher. If the publisher is interested in acquiring the book, the agreement specifies a time period during which the author and the publisher must negotiate as to the terms for publication. If the author and the publisher cannot agree on terms within the specified time period, the author is free to submit the manuscript to other publishers. Under some agreements, if the author and the publisher fail to agree on terms but the author receives an offer from another publisher, the author must bring that offer to the first publisher, and the first publisher will have the right to match or exceed the offer and acquire the book.

The Out of Print Clause

Most publishing agreements contain an "out-of-print" clause that allows the author to regain rights after the publisher has ceased publishing the book. The out-of-print clause should define "out-of-print," and should outline the procedures for the reversion of rights to the author. For example:

- When will a book be deemed to be out-of-print? Possible definitions include: (1) if the book is no longer listed in the publisher's catalog; (2) if there are no copies or less than a specified number of copies available in the publisher's stock; or (3) if no copies or less than a specified number of copies have been sold in the past year.
- Should a book that is available only in electronic or print-on-demand format be deemed to be out-of-print?
- If a book is out-of-print, does the publishing agreement automatically terminate, or is the author required to give the publisher a notice of termination? If the author is required to give a notice, does the agreement terminate upon the giving of that notice, or is the publisher allowed a grace period in which to put the book back in print or to license reprint rights to another publisher?

About David Koehser

612-204-4567

David Koehser represents and advises individuals and businesses on publishing, licensing, copyright, trademark and general business law matters. His clients include publishers, writers, artists, designers, agents and producers. He also works with business consultants and consulting firms, software developers and other retail and service businesses.
He is a past chair of the Minnesota State Bar Association Art & Entertainment Law Section, and the Hennepin County Bar Association Corporate & Business Law Section. He regularly speaks at continuing legal education programs and industry trade group meetings, and has taught publishing law seminars at the University of Minnesota Law School and Hamline University Law School.

Areas of Practice

Publishing

- Publishing Agreements
- Joint Author Collaboration Agreements
- Illustrator Agreements
- Subsidiary Rights License Agreements
- Permissions and Releases
- Agent Agreements
- Distribution Agreements

Merchandise Licensing

- Art, Character, Trademark and Design License Agreements
- Agent Agreements
- Manufacturing and Distribution Agreements

Theatre and Performing Arts

- Theatre Production Agreements
- Theatrical Collaboration Agreements

- Music Licensing
- Talent and Modeling Agreements
- Video Production Agreements
- Film and TV Option and Purchase Agreements

Copyrights and Trademarks

- Copyright Registrations
- Copyright Licenses and Assignments
- Trademark Registrations
- Trademark Licenses and Assignments

Business Law

- New Business Formations
- Purchases and Sales of Existing Businesses
- Consulting Agreements
- Confidentiality and Non-Compete Agreements
- Employment Agreements
- Distribution Agreements

Education

University of Minnesota Law School
J.D. cum laude 1981
University of Iowa
B.A. 1977
Phi Beta Kappa

Bar Admissions

Minnesota 1981
Illinois 1982

Professional Memberships

Minnesota State Bar Association
Business Law Section
Art & Entertainment Law Section (Chair, 1998-1999)
Hennepin County Bar Association
Corporate and Business Law Section (Chair, 1998-1999)
Minnesota Book Publishers Roundtable
Twin Cities Licensing Group

Chapter 6 – Republishing Rights

KNOW YOUR RIGHTS AS THE AUTHOR.

Many authors are clueless when it comes to their rights as a copyrighted author. In this section I have provided an article from The Chicago Press that teaches their journalist exactly what rights they have. This is, again, a very important topic so read slowly and take it all in completely.

http://www.press.uchicago.edu/journals/jrnl_rights.html

The University of Chicago Press Guidelines for Journal Authors' Rights

As a leader in scholarly publishing, the University of Chicago Press has embraced its obligation to disseminate scholarship of the highest standard, to advance scholarly conversation within and across traditional disciplines, and to help define new areas of knowledge and intellectual endeavor. When you publish an article in a journal of the University of Chicago Press or one of its publishing partners, you reap the benefit of a professional publishing house with over a century of commitment to the scholarly enterprise. With our publishing expertise in both traditional and emerging channels of communication, we ensure the widespread distribution of your article throughout the world and to the broadest audience.

The University of Chicago Press supports and encourages our authors' own efforts to promote and disseminate their works. These Guidelines answer the questions we hear most often from our authors about their rights to reuse their articles. Your rights are governed by your Publication Agreement and by the provisions of these Guidelines as in effect at the time of your proposed use of your article. If you have a question that is not addressed here, please contact:

Permissions Department
University of Chicago Press, Journals Division
1427 East 60th Street, Chicago, IL 60637
Email: journalpermissions@press.uchicago.edu

Frequently Asked Questions:

- Do I need to request permission to reuse my article?
- Are there any fees for the reuse of my article?
- Can I post a copy of my article on the Internet?
- Can I post the published version of my article?
- When can I post my article?
- Can I submit my article to an online pre-print or working paper archive?
- Can I submit my article to PubMed Central or PubMed Central UK?
- Can I include my published article, or a pre-publication version, in an institutional repository?
- Can I republish my article in another print publication?
- Can I use my article for teaching purposes in my classes?
- Can I provide copies of my article in print or electronic form to my colleagues?
- Can another author republish my article or a portion thereof without permission?
- What if I included copyrighted material in my article?

Q. Do I need to request permission to reuse my article?

A. You do not need to request permission to reuse your article as described in your Publication Agreement and in these

Guidelines, provided that appropriate credit is given to the journal and you meet all other conditions set out herein. Appropriate credit includes the exact copyright notice as printed in the journal. The form of the copyright notice is: © 2xxx by [name of copyright holder]. For prepublication versions of your article (i.e., pre-prints), appropriate credit means a statement prominently displayed on the paper itself, specifying the paper's status, date, and journal name. (For example: "Submitted (or Accepted) for publication to (by) Journal Name on MM/DD/YYYY.") A link to the journal's home page or the journal article should be included whenever possible.

For uses not described in these Guidelines or in your Publication Agreement or for questions about appropriate credit, please consult the Permissions Department at journalpermissions@press.uchicago.edu.

Please also see the comments at the end of these Guidelines regarding the use of copyrighted material in your article.

Q. Are there any fees for the reuse of my article?

A. There are no fees attached to your reuse of your article according to the terms described in these Guidelines and in the editorial office's communications with you, except that a modest fee may be charged if we supply you with the PDF of your published article.

Q. Can I post a copy of my article on the Internet?

A. In general, you may post a copy of your article on your personal or institutional web server, provided that the server is noncommercial and not intended for the systematic storage, retrieval, and delivery of scholarly material. Appropriate credit should be given to the journal as described previously.

Please note the comments at the end of these Guidelines regarding the use of copyrighted material in your article.

Some journals may place additional conditions on posting. Please review your correspondence or consult the journal's editorial office for details.

Q. Can I post the published version of my article?

A. We encourage you to use or refer to the final, definitive version of your article whenever possible. You have the choice of posting the PDF version of your article or posting the citation, abstract (if present), and a link to the HTML version hosted on the Press's website. You may not, however, post proofs of your article.

Q. When can I post my article?

A. Prior to submission: We place no conditions on posting a paper intended for submission (but not yet submitted) to one of our journals, except to note that posting a paper online may, in some cases, constitute prior publication—for example, posting to a commercial venue and/or to a venue with a formal review and approval process. Please consult the journal's editor if you have questions about whether or not a particular use constitutes prior publication.

Many journals use an anonymous (blind) peer review system. Please be aware that posting a paper intended for submission or submitted to such a journal may compromise the confidentiality of the refereeing process and delay or prevent a decision based on the paper's merits. To find out if posting your paper may compromise the integrity of the peer review process, check the journal's contributor guidelines or consult the journal's editor.

After acceptance: To avoid citation confusion, we discourage online posting of prepublication versions of articles, but in most cases do not restrict posting of a paper accepted for publication provided that the conditions described in these Guidelines have been met. Some journals, however, do not allow prepublication versions to be posted or impose additional restrictions; please consult the journal's editorial office for details.

Upon publication: We encourage you to use or refer to the final, published version of your article on your personal or institutional web server as soon as it is available (remember that articles published by the Press are usually made available online before the print edition is released). Articles posted to an archive or institutional repository, however, may not be made publicly available until the appropriate embargo period has been observed; please see the following sections of these Guidelines for details.

Q. Can I submit my article to an online pre-print or working paper archive?

A. To avoid citation confusion, we discourage online posting of pre-prints and working papers. If you choose to submit a prepublication version of your accepted paper to a noncommercial, discipline-specific preprint or working paper archive, however, we require that appropriate credit be given to the journal as described above and ask you to remove the working paper from the archive after your article is published or replace it with the published version. If you deposit the published version of your article, it may be made publicly available after the appropriate embargo period* has been observed. You are responsible for informing the manager of the archive of the embargo period that must be observed.

Please also note the comments elsewhere in these Guidelines regarding prior publication and anonymous peer review and the use of copyrighted material in your article.

*The embargo period is 12 months.

Q. Can I submit my article to PubMed Central or PubMed Central UK?

A. Authors whose research was funded in whole or in part by the National Institutes of Health (NIH), the Wellcome Trust, or the Medical Research Council (MRC UK) may deposit the accepted manuscript with PubMed Central or PubMed Central UK, with release to the public twelve (12) months after publication for NIH-funded research or six (6) months after publication for Wellcome Trust–funded and Medical Research Council–funded research. Only the final accepted manuscript may be submitted; authors may not submit proofs or the published article to PubMed Central or PubMed Central UK.

Q. Can I include my published article in an official institutional repository?

A. You may place your published article in a *noncommercial* data repository maintained by an institution of which you are a member, provided you meet all relevant conditions described in these Guidelines and in the editorial office's communications with you. An institutional repository, as distinguished from your personal or departmental website, is designed for the systematic storage, retrieval, and delivery of scholarly material. Your article may be made publicly available after the appropriate embargo period* has been observed. You are responsible for informing the manager of the institutional repository of the embargo period that must be observed.

Please also note the comments elsewhere in these Guidelines regarding prior publication and anonymous peer review and the use of copyrighted material in your article.

*The embargo period is 12 months.

Q. Can I republish my article in another print publication?

A. You have the nonexclusive right of republication of your article, in whole or in part, in any book, article, or other scholarly work of which you are an author or an editor, provided that you give credit to the journal, as described earlier in these Guidelines. Please note that the author's right of republication does not apply if the paper is a work-made-for-hire.

Q. Can I use my article for teaching purposes in my classes?

A. You may use your article for teaching purposes in your classes, including making multiple copies for each student, either individually or as part of a printed course pack, provided such course pack will be used solely for classes you teach and provided that such classes are academic and noncommercial in nature (for example, CME courses run by a for-profit organization would not be covered).

Q. Can I provide copies of my article in print or electronic form to my colleagues?

A. You may provide single copies of your article in either print or electronic form to your colleagues for the purposes of scholarly exchange. Copies may not be provided for compensation, for the purposes of republication or preparing derivative works, or as part of the systematic provision of copyrighted material to a third party.

Q. Can another author republish my article or a portion thereof without permission?

A. Your article or portions of your article may be used by other authors in their publications. Small portions may be reprinted without permission from the Press, provided such use falls within the bounds of fair use of copyrighted material. For all other uses, the author and/or publisher must seek permission from the Press.

Q. What if I included copyrighted material in my article?

A. The rights described in these Guidelines pertain only to content for which the University of Chicago Press or one of its publishing partners holds copyright. If you included copyrighted material in your article under fair use provisions, there will be no additional restrictions on further use of the material. If, however, you required permission to include copyrighted material, you must check the permission grant issued by the copyright holder to see if any restrictions apply to your further reuse of the content. It is especially critical to check the permission grants for fine art, video, and audio material, as the use of such material is often restricted to its publication in the journal, and further use of the content, particularly its posting on a freely accessible website, may not be permitted without the explicit permission of the copyright holder.

*****

Okay, as authors of written content, you now are completely armed with the proper and correct information regarding copyright law.

Remember, if you have any questions please write to me: lee.benton@epubwealth.com.

I Have a Special Gift for My Readers

I appreciate my readers for without them I am just another author attempting to make a difference. If my book has made a favorable impression please leave me an honest review. Thank you in advance for you participation.

My readers and I have in common a passion for the written word as well as the desire to learn and grow from books.

My special offer to you is a massive ebook library that I have compiled over the years. It contains hundreds of fiction and non-fiction ebooks in Adobe Acrobat PDF format as well as the Greek classics and old literary classics too.

In fact, this library is so massive to completely download the entire library will require over 5 GBs open on your desktop.

Use the link below and scan all of the ebooks in the library. You can select the ebooks you want individually or download the entire library.

The link below does not expire after a given time period so you are free to return for more books rather than clog your desktop. And feel free to give the link to your friends who enjoy reading too.

I thank you for reading my book and hope if you are pleased that you will leave me an honest review so that I can improve my work and or write books that appeal to your interests.

Okay, here is the link...

http://tinyurl.com/special-readers-promo

PS: If you wish to reach me personally for any reason you may simply write to mailto:support@epubwealth.com.

I answer all of my emails so rest assured I will respond.

Meet the Author

Dr. Leland Benton is Director of Applied Web Info, a holding company for ePubWealth.com, a leading ePublisher company based in Utah. With over 21,000 resellers in over 22-countries, ePubWealth.com is a leader in ePublishing, book promotion, and ebook marketing.

As the creator and author of "The ePubWealth Program," Leland teaches up-and-coming authors the ins-and-outs of today's ePublishing world. He has assisted hundreds of authors make it big in the ePublishing world.

Leland also created a series of external book promotion programs and teaches authors how to promote their books using external marketing sources.

Leland is also the Managing Director of Applied Mind Sciences, the company's mind research unit and Chief Forensics Investigator for the company's ForensicsNation unit. He is active in privacy rights through the company's PrivacyNations unit and is an expert in survival planning and disaster relief through the company's SurvivalNations unit.

Leland resides in Southern Utah.

http://www.amazon.com/author/lelandbenton

Visit some of his websites
http://appliedmindsciences.com/
http://appliedwebinfo.com/
http://BoolbuilderPLUS.com
http://embarrassingproblemsfix.com/
http://www.epubwealth.com/
http://forensicsnation.com/
http://neternatives.com/
http://privacynations.com/
http://survivalnations.com/
http://thebentonkitchen.com
http://theolegions.org

Made in the USA
San Bernardino, CA
03 December 2016